A View To Masonic Education

"The Blue Lodge"

By
A. Keith Jones

Bloomington, IN  Milton Keynes, UK

authorHOUSE

AuthorHouse™
1663 Liberty Drive, Suite 200
Bloomington, IN 47403
www.authorhouse.com
Phone: 1-800-839-8640

AuthorHouse™ UK Ltd.
500 Avebury Boulevard
Central Milton Keynes, MK9 2BE
www.authorhouse.co.uk
Phone: 08001974150

The information provided or advice offered in this manual of Instruction, although based on the author's experience as a active member of this fraternal order, is not intended to substitute for the advice, requirements or counsel of any Grand body of competent jurisdiction. Although most Grand Lodges, if not all, has establish its own particular practices and procedures of similar topics as addressed in this manual, it does offer users of this manual with information that is accredited and established in its generalized content.

First published by AuthorHouse 4/5/2006

ISBN: 1-4259-1247-8 (sc)

Printed in the United States of America
Bloomington, Indiana

This book is printed on acid-free paper.

PREFACE

This Leadership Training manual is based on the idea that there are many members of the Masonic community, young and old, new to the Arts of Masonry and those that have been members of the society for several years or more, who for whatever the reason, do not possess any or much Masonic education. Be it far reaching that informed members of the Masonic Order serves as the backbone for continued growth of the fraternity and that the perpetuation of our existence is dependent on how we as leaders of this time honored organization motivate others in the values that this society can offer for the better construction of that house; ..."not made with hands"

This manual of Instruction has been developed to assist those members with a brief awareness of basic Masonic History, Landmarks, its Constitution, Jurisprudence and Administrative systems. The information presented in this manual of instruction is generalized and does not represent the administration, protocol, operations, functions and procedures of any specific Masonic Grand jurisdiction. Therefore, fraternal members from several jurisdiction may find it useful in there research of Masonic information.

TABLE OF CONTENTS

AUTHENTICATION

The information and material published in this instructional and study manual has been compiled from various sources available covering Masonic information. A portion of the material are extracts from the following publications listed below. This acknowledgement is given for the benefit of future reference to those whom may find it helpful in there further Masonic studies and research. It is not designed to replace any previous published resource or material, it is intended to be used a guide to help those that require a basic laymen's approach to Masonic information.

The accuracy and validity of the information provided can be reviewed by these sources of suggested readings listed and by information published in Grand Lodge bulletins, news letters and other sources. There are a host of other Masonic reading material available through Masonic supply venders and Internet resources. The following list does not limit those interested in furthering their quest for Masonic Information to the ones listed below.

Published Masonic resources:

A New Encyclopedia of Freemasonry   Arthur E. Waite

A Dictionary of Freemasonry   Robert Macoy

Worshipful Master's Assistant   Robert Macoy

The Craft and Its Symbols   Allen E. Roberts

The Meaning of Masonry   W. L. Wilmshurst

Born in Blood   John J. Robinson

The Quest for Light   Wallace Mcleod

Freemasonry and Its Etiquette   William C. Everden

The History of Freemasonry   Albert Mackey

True Masonic Guide   Robert Macoy

Inside Prince Hall   David L. Gray

Introduction to Freemasonry   Michael Poll

INTRODUCTION

"It would be well if we could learn more of what Masonry is than what some think it was." This one statement by Alfred Sawyer made some time ago says it all… For this very reason is my motivation to continue to invest myself with genuine Masonic knowledge; as we say "more light". I extend a warm welcome to all those journeymen who seek to extend their Masonic Knowledge of Freemasonry. Such students, as we all are, in our journey of true "Light", will be encouraged to enter our studies with zeal and thoroughness, that we may more fully enjoy the contents that this course have to offer. It is my hope that this Masonic information and the research committed as well as the subject matter being offered to students in their pursuit will not only challenge them, but will also captivate them with its sheer fascination.

It has been indicated or suggested, whichever the case, by several Masonic authorities and scholars alike, that Freemasonry has been and is on the decline in America, perhaps this is true, yet Masonry continue to thrive and will always find its way to maintain an existence that surpasses any other fraternal organization in America and abroad. Be this as it may, we have much work ahead to restore the reputation of our "Time Honored" institution. Many of us in our youth, before we became members had a hope that some day we, as our fathers and grandfathers had done so, wear the badge of a Mason, walk as proud men, men who captured the envy of our neighbors, men who people looked up to. Where has this gone? What can we do to recapture the enthusiasm and motivation? I suggest one small action, which is to educate ourselves with the basic elements that support this institution. We must learn and/or relearn what and why we are apart and have such an Order. It is sad to say some Brethren are mislead of what Masonry is, what we really stand for, this is caused by the ignorance of other members who do not seek the truth, who lack the will of finding out who and what we are. We can not go into the Lodge rooms and perform the ritualistic works and not expand on why we are there. The Masonic rituals are not the only tools that we have as a resource. Yes, we must learn what is in it, we must also learn how to apply it as well. This is but only one aspect of Masonry. One can spend a life time in research and study of the purpose of Freemasonry, which is the path we as Masons should take in our travels through the stages of life. It is my challenge to all to continue to expand his own knowledge outside of this manual of instruction, cause others see the beauty that a well informed Brother can exert. The enthusiasm will be a necessary element to cultivate the success in our aim to play a part in fortifying members of the craft in Freemasonry through Knowledge. Each of us has set out on a journey to seek the knowledge that may better able us to apply ourselves to an ability to serve. Whatever to its extinct, that at the end of the day, or when we come to the end of the road of life, and there we stand before the Judge of all judges, the giver of all good things, that we have so enjoyed during the tenure of our watch, that we may be blessed with a pass to the "right", as we begin to enjoy the rewards of our labor from a seat in the "East".

Bro. Tony K. Jones, 33°, PM
President, Past Master's Council
Special Deputy, MWGL of Tennessee
2004-2005

THE PURPOSE OF FREEMASONRY

<u>What is the purpose of Masonry?</u> One of its most basic purposes is to make good men even better. We try to place emphasis on the individual man by strengthening his character, improving his moral and spiritual outlook, and broadening his mental horizons. We try to impress upon the minds of our members the principles of personal responsibility and morality, encouraging each member to practice in his daily life the lessons taught through symbolic ceremonies in the lodge. One of the universal doctrines of Freemasonry is the belief in the "Brotherhood of Man and the Fatherhood of God". The importance of this belief is established by each Mason as he practices the three principle tenets of Masonry: Brotherly Love, Relief and Truth.

Masonry is also the custodian of a tradition of initiation. It is the duty of every Freemason to preserve and perpetuate this tradition for future ages. This is a heavy responsibility and should give pause to any who would seek to make changes in the body of the Craft, except those with the highest motives and deepest understanding of the principles involved.

CHAPTER 1

The Purpose of Masonic Education

And

History of the Craft

"A Closer Look"

MASONIC EDUCATION

"The lack of educational work in the average Lodge is the principal reason for the lack of interest and the consequent poor membership attendance, over which spokesman have been wringing their hands for at least a century". This quote stirs one to think about the importance and value of Masonic education within the Masonic Fraternity. It should further stir us to think about why this important aspect of Freemasonry has been so badly overlooked. We must not kid ourselves into thinking that Masonic education is playing the prominent part in Freemasonry, that by right it should. This leads to the all important question, "Why has this situation come about?" The real problem in trying to answer this question is that there is no easy answer. We, as a Fraternity, have reached the point where far too few of our members have even the faintest idea of why they are Freemasons, let alone, have any real knowledge about its history and heritage. The surprising notion is Masonic Education is not a new kid on the block, it has always existed. To those of you who are "ritual purists" please do not let my next statement shock you, but the real truth of the matter is we have come to depend on the ritual as the basis for Masonic knowledge. The ritual does not make Masons. It only makes members! We cheat, wrong and defraud any candidate who is left hanging at the end of the 3rd Degree, having heard a lot of words and really not knowing what they mean. Ask yourself this, "Is his plate full"? Until the Degrees are explained to the candidate, he has no idea of what he has gone through. To suggest that the explanation is complete with the lectures of each Degree is again burying our head in the proverbial "Masonic Sand."

Let me stress no one loves the ritual more than I do. The ritual has an important place in the life of the person who is becoming a Mason. But, that place is not the "throne from on high" from which there is no more to learn. In my opinion, it is far easier to memorize and recite the ritual than it is to study and understand the meaning of it. So, we tend to be far more comfortable in working the Degrees than in working with the candidate to teach him what our beautiful craft represents. Has this always been so? The answer, of course, is no. But we (or a some of us) have drifted so far away from true knowledge within our Fraternity that now it is very difficult to try to turn the tide. But we are going to have to do that very thing! What are in fact the origins of Freemasonry? Where did it begin? How did it reach the present state in which we find it today? Wouldn't it be wonderful if we could answer these questions in ten words or less. We can not. We can only surmise what in fact may have happened. Historically, of course, Freemasonry did not begin with the forming of a Grand Lodge in London in 1717. Quite obviously, there had to have been Lodges to be formed at that time. So, they must have had some history prior to that date. When did it all begin? We simply don't know.

One thing has always bothered me with the explanation we are usually given. That is: Why did the ancient Guilds of Cathedral builders need such an elaborate method of recognition? Why would they have needed signs and words, if in fact our early origins were with tradesmen applying their skill in building cathedrals? That they would wish to keep secret the method by which they constructed a building might perhaps be possible. But, they were out in the open, visible to anyone who wished to come near the building and certainly not in any danger from any outside or enemy from within. So why would they need to have methods of recognition that would not have been known to the casual observer? This question has always intrigued me. Please let me tell you right now, I do not know the answer. One of the better theories that I have read concerning this matter is in a book by John Robinson entitled, Born in Blood.

Let me just say briefly that his theory is that Freemasonry very likely began with the suppression of the Knights Templar in the year 1307. At that time the Templars were crushed in France, but by the delay of the King in enforcing the edict in England and Scotland many escaped. It is Mr. Robinson's theory that they went underground and had to devise a method of recognition enabling them to travel safely and to establish safe houses where they would have an opportunity to rest and refresh themselves. It also gave them the ability to recognize each other as members of the order! While the suppression of the Knights Templar may or may not have anything to do with early Freemasonry, it certainly makes more sense to me that secret signs and words in this type of environment were far more necessary than with the simple workman applying his trade in building a cathedral. Just one more thought from this particular theory. The suppression of the Knights Templar occurred on October 13, 1307. The particular day of the week was a Friday and ever since that event Friday the 13th has been considered to be the unluckiest day of the year.

Now, the suppression of the Templars was crude and bloody but it was not an unusual event in those times. War, pillage, and confiscation of property were a way of life. There were other orders in existence who had their troubles as well. What was there about the Knights Templar that made them known and recognized and respected? Why do I say respected? Because there wasn't any rejoicing at their suppression. Instead the day is remembered as unlucky! The only conclusion that I can reach is that this order held the respect of the people and their destruction brought about the omen of bad luck. Why were they so respected? Obviously, there is no absolute answer to that question, but one could surmise that if they were indeed practicing the principles of Freemasonry they would certainly have had the respect of the people My conclusion is that Freemasonry has existed for a very long time. Not perhaps, as we know it today, but as an order of men doing good work where they were permitted to exist. This observation is not to be taken in the context of the claims of many Masonic writers, such as: Masonry goes back to the times of Solomon or even Noah and the flood. In Masonic writing we must be very careful when making claims like this. Many times ancient symbols, which have in more recent times been co-opted by Freemasonry, are mistaken as evidence of early Masonic existence .Let me give you one example. The All Seeing Eye on the one dollar bill is certainly well known in Masonic circles and, unfortunately, has mistakenly been interpreted as a Masonic symbol. It is in fact an ancient symbol which was taken into Freemasonry in far more recent times.

This lack of understanding of ancient signs and symbols has, in my judgment, misled many Masonic historians into false conclusions. The study of history, particularly, where the written word was not used requires a well trained Brother when interpreting its meaning. That is why we need to do a far better job of interpreting early Masonic history than we have done in the past. If Masonic history began in earlier times than we normally talk about, it is obviously going to make a reconstruction of our past difficult because we have very few written records to go by. Remember these were times when few people could read or write. So, we don't have minutes of early Lodge meetings available. Also remember, if their very lives were at stake, that was another strong inducement not to put very much information into written form!

The purpose of my tracing this obscure part of our history is simply to say to you that I very strongly believe that there was a far more significant purpose to the origins of Freemasonry than simply erecting buildings! I do believe that Freemasonry evolved into that stage, during its development, but the Cathedral builders reflected a time in our history and not its beginning! Let me carry this thinking one step further and bring it into the late 1700's. Benjamin Franklin and Voltaire did not join a workers guild! They joined what they believed to be an educational society which was called, "Freemasonry." These were extremely intelligent men who had no time to waste on things that were not important to them, and yet Franklin was an active Freemason and Voltaire joined only shortly before his death! What was it that they saw in Freemasonry that eludes us today? Well let's focus our thoughts more on modern Freemasonry and see what we can determine. It has been said that Freemasonry in Europe was for the elite and in America for the masses. With the great numbers of members that we have attracted over the years, there seems to be a certain amount of truth in that statement. Today we tend to overlook the fact that even though our numbers are dwindling we still have in excess of two and one-half million Freemasons in the United States alone. It would seem that when Freemasonry caught fire it did so in massive numbers. In the 1920's we were in the three millions in membership. In the 1950's and early 60's in the four millions and have been on a decline ever since. But, if we look at the membership in the 1700's, when by any standard of measurement Freemasonry was certainly at its most influential peak, there were not very many Freemasons! Lodges were small, intimate and every Brother knew every other Brother. With larger numbers, perhaps also, came the seeds of our own downfall. It is very difficult to have personal knowledge of each Brother when our numbers are so large. One of the most frequent complaints we hear in Freemasonry is a Brother saying that "I was in the hospital and no one came to see me. The chances are no one even knew he was in the hospital! We also have an extremely mobile population. It is no exaggeration to say that somewhere in the 30% range of the members of each Grand Lodge live somewhere else, other than the Jurisdiction in which they where raised. How do you keep a personal relationship with a Brother when you don't even know where he is?

It would seem to me that one of the greatest mistakes we have made in Freemasonry is to try to run it as we did in the 1700's. You can't run an organization with a few thousand members the same way as you do one with millions of members. It just can't be done! We did not develop, through Masonic education, the training programs, the communication, the leadership that was necessary to deal with these vast numbers. When we talk about the "old days" when all of the leading men of the town were in Freemasonry we overlook the fact that the town was very small and everybody knew everyone else. Now we have vast cities where people don't know everyone else. Yet we still think of Masonry in terms of those earlier times. It's impossible not to conclude that we simply have to do a much better job of communicating with and educating our membership!

It is no secret that we have thousands upon thousands of books on Masonry and for the most part the one thing they have in common is that they are, for the most part unread. We have to find a way of developing material that will be used in the Masonic community. Realistically we have to get right down to the Blue Lodge Level and insist that every Lodge must offer a course in Masonic education. If they don't have the resources within the Lodge to provide that education then it must be done either by another Lodge or at the district level. We can no longer turn out members who do not know anything about our Fraternity. The price we are paying for that mistake is clearly evident today! Programs can be developed but it does require commitment on the part of the Grand Lodge, but more importantly, commitment on the part of knowledgeable Masons within each Lodge who will actively accept the responsibility to see that all Masons are properly taught about the Fraternity. Certainly Grand Lodges can be of tremendous help in developing a program common to all Lodges within their Jurisdiction a program that would be at least enough to entice the appetite of the members so that they would want to do more on their own to learn and teach themselves basic Masonic information! During a recent study by the Masonic Renewal Task Force, one of the issues that kept repeating itself over and over again was the lack of interest by our present members. The membership of Freemasonry can really be divided into three groups. If you will, imagine three side by side circles, the largest circle being the base which is the greatest percentage of our membership and largely inactive, a smaller circle in the middle which would be the body with a somewhat active membership; and the tiniest circle of all, the head, with the smallest group of Masons and the most active.

It is with the large, inactive base that our attention should be directed. The deaths occurring are roughly the same in number as the new members being brought in, so one offsets the other. Where we are losing our members is in the two categories of non-Payment of dues and demits. Surveys have shown that of this very large base of membership, when asked why they pay their dues, 33% responded "to maintain membership" and 15% didn't even know why! These are the ones who, through lack of interest, are now leaving Freemasonry. This group I believe represents the residue of the "aura of Freemasonry" that used to say to a man "You Should Belong." Many joined believing this. Now we have a group of men who never quite knew why they joined and over the years have never found out why, have reached that point where, either through lack of interest, or cutting back financially have no incentive to remain in Masonry. They have been around for years and have never been active and now see no need to stay a member. We are losing that group. We are not replacing them and unless and until we can find a way to communicate intelligently with them and show them a reason why being a Freemason is important they will continue to drift away. It is inevitable! But the good news is we can do something about this situation! We can do something about lack of interest and that my Brothers is the challenge facing Freemasonry today! At the very least inactive members should be invited to attend the instructional classes for new members that we have already talked about. Let me not present Freemasonry as all doom and gloom. It most certainly is not.

We have a tremendous amount of good work going for us. Let me share with you some words from a May 1991, Short Talk Bulletin entitled, "And The Greatest Of These Is Charity." This quote is from that Short Talk Bulletin which was written by S. Brent Morris, a well known Masonic author: "A study of Masonic Charities is a study of the evolving needs of the American society. When food and shelter were immediate and almost daily concerns, Masons responded with firewood and the fruits of their harvests. When care of the aged, widows, and orphans were worries, Masons erected retirement homes and orphanages. When education was needed, Masons built schools, and when these basic needs moved ever farther from common experience, Masons turned their philanthropy to crippled children, burn victims, the speech and language impaired, cancer patients, and others."

It is very clear that when Masons are challenged, they will respond! These are visible challenges of people needing help. Now we must accept the invisible challenge of Masons needing greater understanding of the history and purposes of the Craft! Perhaps Freemasonry could never be more graphically described than in another quote from a Short Talk Bulletin. This one is entitled, "Ellis Island - The Golden Door" and was written by a man who is not a Mason, Mr. Dennis Hearn. Mr. Hearn worked very closely with members of the Grand Lodge of New York and did a great deal of research into the history of Freemasonry as the Ellis Island project developed. His association with Masons led him to this conclusion: "The Freemasons among our Founding Fathers brought to their work the ancient Masonic Landmarks of Truth and Brotherly love, and they fashioned a constitution which, by the depth and strength of its conviction, embedded those principles in the conscience of a nation. While we as a people have not always lived up to them, neither have we been able to ignore them. "Those are very beautiful words to describe Freemasonry. Isn't it time we reintroduced ourselves to the meaning of Freemasonry and got back to living and practicing this beautifully descriptive picture of our order?

GENERAL HISTORY OF FREEMASONRY

" *Of all the institutions which have been established for the purpose of improving the conditions of mankind, freemasonry stands preeminent in usefulness as it is in age*". Its origin is lost in the abyss of unexplored antiquity. No historical record, no traditional accounts, can with certainty point out the precise time, the place or the particular manner of its commencement. While some have endeavored to discover its footsteps amongst the master-builders and artist engaged in the construction of the first Jewish temple, others have attempted to trace it to the Eleusian mysteries, which are said to have taught the immortality of the soul and the other sublime truths of natural religion. Some again have ascribed its rise to the sainted heroes of the Crusades; while others have endeavored to penetrate the mysteries of the Druids, and to discover its origin amongst the wise men of that institution."

DeWitt Clinton

The difficulty of arriving at the precise time, place or circumstance in which Masonry or its true prototype began, has been encountered by every writer upon the subject. Some, over-anxious for the dignity of the fraternity, have represented it as coeval with the world. Others, more moderate, find its origin in the religious mysteries of the ancient world,

11

and particularly in a supposed branch of those religious associations formed by the architects of Tyre, who, under the name "DIONYSIAC FRATERNITY," constituted an association of builders, exclusively engaged in the construction of temples and other prominent edifices in Asia Minor, and who were distinguished by the use of secret signs and other modes of mutual recognition. Without adopting any untenable opinions, we are justified in avowing that the institution must have been framed by a people who had made considerable advance in science.

"In the beginning, GOD created the heavens and the earth. The earth was without form, and void. And darkness was upon the face of the deep. And the spirit of GOD moved upon the face of the waters, and GOD said: 'Let There Be Light", and there was light. This quote from Genesis 1:1-3 is powerful, and also ironic that it is also what every masonic candidate hears during his entrance. It is suiting for all new members start their path of Brotherly Love, Relief and Truth, with the word of GOD.

OPERATIVE and SPECULATIVE MASONS

Operative Masons

Most people have never heard of these terms. Operative Masons were essentially individuals whose trade was working with stone. The Speculative Masons were individuals who wanted to be a part of the Stone Mason Guild, but they did not wish to learn the trade.

In 1390 the oldest existing Masonic manuscript called the Regius Poem was written. Throughout Europe giant Gothic cathedrals were being built. The guild system was still very popular in the civilized nations. The guild system offered training for the youth. In return for their education they had to serve in a guild and under a Master for many years. In order to protect the trade against shoddy workmen and cheap laborers they bound themselves together, often under severe oaths, to keep the secrets of the trade at all costs.

In an age when tradesmen of all classes were pulling together into guilds, it would have been most unusual if the stone masons had not followed suite. We do know that such guilds did exist. When the Exeter Cathedral was built in 1396 it term "Freemasons" was mentioned. In 1537 the London guild of stone workers called itself "Freemasons."

During the Cathedral Age the Masons formed themselves in workmen's Guilds; each Guild forming a Lodge with regular officers and with three degrees of Membership. The first group were apprentices or bearers of burdens, the second were craftsmen or skilled workmen on the Temples and the third were Masters or superintendents of the structures being built.

In order to advance to a higher position each guild member had to obtain certain proficiencies in his work. As he advanced he learned certain attributes of moral conduct. Some believe that it was these guilds that developed into our modern Masonic Lodges.

A Mason was called a Freemason because he was not born into slavery, he had the freedom to travel where ever he wished to work. Another plus for him was that he was sometimes free from paying taxes. Due to all of these distinctions and the fact that he was very skillful in his trade, he was called a Freemason. Speculative Masons

Most of the great Gothic buildings were completed in the 16th century. For some reason the demand for these structures were dwindling. The Guild Lodges were struggling to maintain their existence. The Operative Masons, who found the guilds to be a vital part of their trade had also come to love the rituals, teachings, and fellowship that they found in their guild Lodges. Fearing that the guild would soon pass into obsolescence they had to consider different ways of keeping the Lodge active. There were certain people who saw virtue and honor in belonging to the Lodge and soon they were welcomed into the Lodges as Speculative members.

Speculative Masons

Many of these new members were teachers, mathematicians, artist and poets. When the Lodges began to accept these new members it was said that they were Free and Accepted Masons. The Lodge was slowly transforming from a focus on a skilled trade to a focus on the moral principles and discipline that was found in the Lodge. New members were accepted into the Lodge but they still had to learn the old rituals of conferring degrees and had to same obligations as the Operative Masons had.

There is much speculation today that Speculative Masonry began in the 15th century, especially in France, England, and Scotland. It has been theorized that many of the banished Knights Templars found a new purpose in the guilds. John J. Robinson, one of the best Masonic writers of recent times feels very strongly that the Templars had a very strong influence on modern Masonry. My own theory is that Masonry was born in a secret society formed for self-protection by fugitive Knights Templar, along with their employees and their associates, England and Scotland, who had been found guilty of heresy and excommunicated by Pope Clement V. With their order destroyed by papal decree and themselves branded as excommunicated outlaws, the Templars who managed to escape were in extreme peril. If found, their fate would undoubtedly include torture and burning at the stake. They had a vital need for passwords, recognition signals, and secret meetings.

During the ensuing years (after the Inquisition), the one secret that a man could have had that would cost him his life and property was that he had material disagreement with the Church of Rome, and so could be convicted of heresy.... When revealing oneself could bring such physical and economic tragedy, any man can be expected to demand all the protection from betrayal that he can get. That is why candidates for membership in the society were blindfolded until they had taken their oaths to keep their brother's secrets.... Since even to be spotted attending a clandestine meeting might mean betrayal and death, a lookout or sentry was always posted when members gathered. Freemasons remember that function with the lodge officer called the Tyler... To help a brother on the run from the threat of torture and death, it was essential to have a system of words and signs of recognition that cold be used wherever the Mason might find himself.

Within few generations the Speculative Masons (be they Knight Templars or not) were growing in strength and the Operative Masons were slowly dying out. Eventually, the Lodge would consist of only Speculative Masons. The Operatives were gone, their traditions remained. The Speculatives would become Entered Apprentices, then Fellow Crafts, and finally Master Masons.

AFRICAN AMERICANS IN MASONRY

Prince Hall
1735 –1807
Founder and Father of African American
Masonry in the United States

Prince Hall, one of Boston's most prominent citizens during the revolutionary period, was the founder of the African Lodge of the Honorable Society of Free and Accepted Masons of Boston, the world's first lodge of black Freemasonry and the first society in American history devoted to social, political, and economic improvement. Not much is known of Hall's life before the Revolution. He was born in 1735 and was the slave of William Hall of Boston. His son, Primus, was born in 1756 to Delia, a servant in another household. In 1762, at the age of 27, Hall joined the Congregational Church, and soon after, married an enslaved woman named Sarah Ritchie. Eight years later, after Sarah's death, he married Flora Gibbs of Gloucester. A month after the Boston Massacre, William Hall freed Prince; his certificate of manumission read that he was "no longer Reckoned a slave, but [had] always accounted as a free man." Hall made his living as a huckster (peddler), caterer and leather dresser, and was listed as a voter and a taxpayer. He owned a small house and leather workshop in Boston. It is believed that he was one of the six black men of Massachusetts named Prince Hall listed in military records of the Revolution, and he may well have fought at Bunker Hill. A bill he sent to a Colonel Crafts indicates that he crafted five leather drumheads for the Boston Regiment of Artillery in April, 1777.

As the archives reflect and the records show, a significant event occurred on March 6, 1775. An Army Sgt., by the name of John Batt, working under the authority and Constitution of the Grand Lodge of Ireland, initiated Prince Hall and fourteen (14) other free Black men into Masonry in Army Lodge No. 44. The other candidates were Cyrus Johnson, Bueston Slinger, Prince Rees, John Canton, Peter Freeman, Benjamin Tiler, Duff Ruform, Thomas Santerson, Prince Rayden, Cato Speain, Boston Smith, Peter Best, Forten Howard and Richard Titley. When the British Regiments left Boston on March 17, 1776, a Dispensation was issued by Batt authorizing Prince Hall and his Brethren to meet as a Lodge under restrictions. Under this Permit, African Lodge No. 1 was formed July 3, 1776. Official acknowledgment of the legitimacy of African Lodge No. 1 was almost immediately made by John Rowe of Boston, a Caucasian and Provincial Grand Master of North America holding authority from the premier Grand Lodge of Freemasons, the Grand Lodge of England, he too, also issued a permit authorizing African Lodge No. 1 to appear publicly in procession as a Masonic Body for the purpose of Celebrating the Feast of Saints John and to bury its dead.

For nine (9) years these Brethren, with other free black men who had received their degrees in Europe, assembled together and enjoyed their limited privileges as Masons, distressed that Prince Hall's attempt to formally associate African Lodge with Caucasian Grand Lodges were frustrated by bigotry and racism. It was an ironic period in American history when colonist embraced the doctrine of independence, liberty, and equality to justify the revolt against English rule while promoting and condoning the economic and social exploitation of Blacks debased by slavery. Finally, in March, 1784, Prince Hall petitioned the Grand Lodge of England through Worshipful Master William Moody of Brotherly Love Lodge No. 55 (London, England) for a Warrant of Constitution. The Charter was prepared and issued on September 29, 1784, although it would be three before African Lodge could actually receive it, the reason for this delay was unclear to its exact nature, however, Prince Hall was informed that the initial payment for the Dispensation was not received with the original petition. Therefore Prince Hall solicited the assistance of Brother and Captain James Scott, whom was given the monies for said Dispensation. Brother Moody sent a letter to Prince Hall on March 10, 1787, informing him that the Charter issued by the Grand Lodge of England was delivered to Captain James Scott of the ship Neptune and Brother-in-law of John Hancock, one of the signers of the Constitution and President of the Continental Congress. The Charter, signed by Deputy Grand Master Roland Holt and witness by Grand Secretary William White, Reconstituted African Lodge No. 1 as African Lodge No. 459 and thus began the parallel lines of Black and Caucasian Freemasonry which continues to exist in America, to this very day. Some white Masons say that Blacks were not denied admission to white Lodges and they point to the very few and the presence of others by invitation as proofs. D Bentley, a contemporary who wrote in his diary, available to all, "The truth is they are ashamed of being equal with Blacks. Even the fraternities of France, given to merit without distinction of color do not influence Massachusetts's Masons to give an embrace less emphatically or tender affectionate to their Black Brethren. It is evident that a preeminence is claimed by whites. The same situation exists in America today but not in all States. Many Caucasian Masons refuse to recognize Prince Hall masons, However, they do consider permitting a limited number of Black men, thought to be prestigious and financially solvent, to become members of their Lodges. Before 1815, exclusive territorial jurisdiction was not an active and recognized doctrine of English Masonic customs. The African lodge of Boston exercised its right to establish other Lodges, making its self a Mother Lodge, its Master prince Hall having the authority to issue warrants on the same basis as Masters of Lodges in Europe!

African Lodges were constituted in Pennsylvania, Rhode Island and New York. On June 24, 1791, the African Grand Lodge of North America was Organized in Boston with Prince Hall as Grand Master. This was one (1) year before the organization of the United Grand Lodge of Massachusetts (Caucasian). In 1827, 45 years after the Caucasian Grand Lodge of Massachusetts had done so, African Lodge of Boston declared itself independent of the Grand Lodge of England.

THE CHARTER ISSUED BY THE GRAND LODGE OF ENG-
LAND TO AFRICAN LODGE No. 459, IS THE **ONLY KNOWN
CHARTER ISSUED BY ANY GRAND BODY EMPOWERED
TO ISSUE SUCH A DOCUMENT,** THE **GRAND LODGE OF
ENGLAND, OF THIS PERIOD, TO BE IN EXISTANCE, TO
THIS VERY DAY!!!**

Prince Hall was appointed a Provincial Grand Master in 1791 by
H.R.H., the Prince of Wales. The question of extending Masonry arose
when Absalom Jones of Philadelphia, Pennsylvania appeared in Boston.
He was an ordained Episcopal priest and a mason who was interested
in establishing a masonic lodge in Philadelphia. Under the authority
of the charter of African Lodge #459, Prince Hall established African
Lodge #459 of Philadelphia on March 22, 1797 and Hiram Lodge #3
in Providence, Rhode Island on June 25, 1797.

African Lodge of Boston became the "Mother Lodge" of the Prince Hall
Family. It was typical for new lodges to be established in this manner
in those days. The African Grand Lodge was not organized until 1808
when representatives of African Lodge #459 of Boston, African Lodge

#459 of Philidelphia and Hiram Lodge #3 of Providence met in New York City.

Upon Prince Hall's death on December 4, 1807, Nero Prince became Master. When Nero Prince sailed to Russia in 1808, George Middleton succeeded him. After Middleton, Peter Lew, Samuel H. Moody and then, John T. Hilton became Grand Master. In 1827, Hilton recommended a Declaration of Independence from the English Grand Lodge.

African Lodge #459 continued until March, 1848, when the Lodge was split to form three Lodges: Union Lodge #2, Celestial Lodge #3 and The Rising Sons of St. John #4, just after the Grand Lodge changed its name to <u>Prince Hall Grand Lodge</u>, honoring its founder and first Grand Master, Prince Hall. Today, styled 47 Most Worshipful Prince Hall Grand Lodges with over 4,500 lodges, can trace their roots to African Lodge # 459, forming 47 independent jurisdictions with a membership of well over 300,000 masons worldwide.

MOST WORSHIPFUL PRINCE HALL GRAND LODGES, U.S.A.

- Most Worshipful Prince Hall Grand Lodge F&AM of Alabama
- Most Worshipful Prince Hall Grand Lodge of Alaska
- Most Worshipful Prince Hall Grand Lodge of Arizona and Jurisdiction
- Most Worshipful Prince Hall Grand Lodge of Arkansas
- Most Worshipful Prince Hall Grand Lodge of California, Inc.
- Most Worshipful Prince Hall Grand Lodge of Colorado & Jurisdiction
- Most Worshipful Prince Hall Grand Lodge of Connecticut
- Most Worshipful Prince Hall Grand Lodge F&AM of Delaware
- Most Worshipful Prince Hall Grand Lodge F&AM, District of Columbia
- Most Worshipful Union Grand Lodge of Florida & Belize, Central America (PHA)
- Most Worshipful Prince Hall Grand Lodge of Georgia

A. KEITH JONES

- Most Worshipful Prince Hall Grand Lodge F&AM, Hawaii and Jurisdiction

- Most Worshipful Prince Hall Grand Lodge of Illinois and Jurisdiction

- Most Worshipful Prince Hall Grand Lodge F&AM of Indiana

- Most Worshipful Prince Hall Grand Lodge of Iowa and Jurisdiction

- Most Worshipful Prince Hall Grand Lodge of Kansas and Jurisdiction

- Most Worshipful Prince Hall Grand Lodge of Kentucky

- Most Worshipful Prince Hall Grand Lodge of Louisiana and Jurisdiction

- Most Worshipful Prince Hall Grand Lodge of Maryland and Jurisdiction, Inc.

- Most Worshipful Prince Hall Grand Lodge of Massachusetts

- Most Worshipful Prince Hall Grand Lodge of Michigan

- Most Worshipful Prince Hall Grand Lodge of Minnesota and Jurisdiction

- Most Worshipful Prince Hall Grand Lodge of Missouri and Jurisdiction

- Most Worshipful Prince Hall Grand Lodge of Nebraska and Jurisdiction

- Most Worshipful Prince Hall Grand Lodge of Nevada

- Most Worshipful Prince Hall Grand Lodge F&AM State of New Jersey

- Most Worshipful Prince Hall Grand Lodge of New Mexico

- Most Worshipful Prince Hall Grand Lodge of New York
- Most Worshipful Prince Hall Grand Lodge of North Carolina
- Most Worshipful Prince Hall Grand Lodge of Ohio F&AM
- Most Worshipful Prince Hall Grand Lodge of Oklahoma
- Most Worshipful Prince Hall Grand Lodge of Oregon
- Most Worshipful Prince Hall Grand Lodge of Pennsylvania
- Most Worshipful Prince Hall Grand Lodge of the State of Rhode Island
- Most Worshipful Prince Hall Grand Lodge of South Carolina
- Most Worshipful Prince Hall Grand Lodge F&AM of Tennessee
- Most Worshipful Prince Hall Grand Lodge of Texas and Jurisdiction
- Most Worshipful Prince Hall Grand Lodge of Virginia
- Most Worshipful Prince Hall Grand Lodge of Washington
- Most Worshipful Prince Hall Grand Lodge of West Virginia
- Most Worshipful Prince Hall Grand Lodge of Wisconsin

GENERAL INFORMATION

FREEMASONRY DEFINED:

What is the definition of Freemasonry? In old England, it was defined as "a system of morality, veiled in allegory (or a story) and illustrated by symbols." It is a course of moral instruction which uses both allegories and symbols to teach its lessons. The modern definition is "Freemasonry is an organized society of men, symbolically applying the principles of Operative Masonry and architecture to the science and art of character building." In other words, we are trying to use the old methods to make good men better.

THE PURPOSE OF FREEMASONRY:

What is the purpose of Masonry? One of the most basic purposes is to make "Better men out of good man" We try to place emphasis on the individual man by strengthening his character; improving his moral and spiritual outlook; and broadening his mental horizons. We try to impress upon the minds of our members the principles of personal responsibility and morality; teaching each member to practice in his daily life the lessons taught through symbolic ceremonies in the lodge. One of the universal doctrines of Freemasonry is the belief in the "Brotherhood of Man and the Fatherhood of God". **The importance** of this belief is established by each Mason as he practices the three principle tenets of Masonry: Brotherly Love, Relief and Truth.

ORIGIN OF FREEMASONRY:

How did Freemasonry originate? We are not sure at what point in time our craft was born. We do know it goes far beyond written record and we believe it was not always called Freemasonry. Some of the ancient mysteries of Egypt, Greece and the Orient influenced our ceremonies that are used today. These ceremonies were designed to test men and to admit only those who were worthy. Our ceremonies are somewhat the same - only of a less physical nature, and in a more spiritual form.

THE TRANSITION FROM OPERATIVE TO SPECULATIVE MASONRY:

What is the difference between "Operative" and "Speculative" Masonry? Operative refers to the time in our history where Masons actually did the physical labor of building. They were the best at their craft, and they kept secret their methods of building. **Speculative refers to the period of time when men were accepted into the Craft as "non-operative" members. They were not "physical builders", but "builders of character" instead.**

ORIGIN OF THE FIRST GRAND LODGE:

By the first part of the 18th century, there were many lodges in England. By the year 1716 A.D., most of the lodges had only non-operative members. In December of 1716, on St. John's Day, a number of members met in London and had an informal meeting. As a result of this meeting, the members of the four Lodges met again in London on **June 24, 1717 A.D.** and formed the first Grand Lodge. **This became one of the most important dates in Masonic history because it marked the start of**

modern Freemasonry as we know it today. With the exception of a few Lodges, every regular Masonic Lodge today was granted a charter or warrant from a Grand Lodge. Every Grand Lodge has a certain jurisdiction or an area to represent. In the United States, every State and the District of Columbia is governed by a Grand Lodge.

TITLES OF GRAND LODGES - F. & A. M. and A. F. & A. M.:

Titles of Grand Lodges in the United States also vary. Some are called A. F. & A. M. which means Ancient Free and Accepted Masons. The other most commonly used title is F. & A. M., or Free and Accepted Masons. The reason for this difference is that in England, when Grand Lodges first started, there was a rivalry between the Irish faction and the English faction - much like there is, yet, today. One faction adopted the Ancient title and the other did not. This carried over to the United States, and we still have both titles in existence. Two other titles exist in America. South Carolina Masons call themselves Ancient Free Masons or A. F. M., the only jurisdiction so designated in the United States. The District of Colombia Masons call themselves Free Ancient and Accepted Masons, or F. A. & A. M., but, no matter what the title, all Lodges work toward the same goals. In California, they call themselves F. & A. M, Free and Accepted Masons, as with most if not all Masons of the Prince Hall Jurisdiction.

THE TITLE OF "FREE AND ACCEPTED":

How did the words "Free" and "Accepted" originate? The ancient craftsmen were very skilled, and their craft was considered to be indispensable to the welfare of both "Church" and "State". For this reason, they were not placed under the same restrictions as were other workers - they were "free" to do their work, travel and live their lives in a manner which befitted their importance. Back in old England, this type of behavior was rare. Most workers were under bond to the owners of the land on which they worked. We believe this freedom for the Operative Mason dates back to the year 946, in York, England. The word "Accepted" also goes back to the time of the Operative Mason. During the latter years of the Middle Ages, there were few educated men outside the monasteries of the world. Naturally, men wanted to become Freemasons to obtain the advantages the craft had to offer. These men did not, necessarily, want to build buildings; they wanted to belong to the organization. These were "Accepted" Masons, rather than "Operative" Masons. This practice, probably originated when some of the people, for whom craftsmen were working, asked to be admitted and, therefore, the practice grew with time. This was a big boost to Masonry, because the secrets of building trades were becoming more widely-known, architecture was changing and our membership was declining. By becoming "speculative" the Craft grew rapidly. As time went on, there became many more "accepted" members than there were operative members and eventually we became a speculative rather than an operative organization.

IS FREEMASONRY A SECRET SOCIETY?:

The answer is: "NO". A secret society is one in which the membership is concealed; the meeting places are kept secret; and knowledge of its organization and principles is unknown to the public. We have a few secrets in Freemasonry - a part of our ritual, our modes of recognition and the business of the Lodge. Portions of our ritual have been handed down within Freemasonry for centuries and form a part of our traditions. However, our purposes, ideals and principles may be learned by anyone who inquires. There are numerous books on these subjects available to the public. All printed Masonic information, with the exception of our esoteric work, may be freely discussed in public. We wear lapel pins and Masonic jewelry, march in parades as Masons with our distinctive aprons, advertise the time and place of our meetings, and openly sponsor charities. We can hardly be called a secret society. Yes, we have some secrets, but no more so than most other fraternities or even families.

IS FREEMASONRY A RELIGION?:

Again, the answer is "NO". Because of the nature of the teachings of Freemasonry, we do ask our candidates to acknowledge a belief and trust in God. Otherwise the ceremonies would be meaningless. But we do not require that you belong to a particular religion or a particular church. An atheist can not become a Mason because he can not express a belief in a Supreme Being.

Religion is defined as:

1. Belief in a divine or superhuman power or powers to be obeyed and worshipped as the creator and ruler of the universe.

2. Expression of this belief in conduct and ritual.

3. Any specific system of belief, worship conduct, etc., often involving a code of ethics and a philosophy.

Masonry, like all its teachings, is not set forth in written creeds. The Mason must come upon it for himself and put it in such form as will satisfy his own mind, leaving others to do likewise. This is Masonic tolerance, one of the prime principles of the Craft, and protected by the Old Charge which forbids all sectarian discussion in our assemblies. Our Order seeks only to unite good men for the purpose of brotherhood - not to promote a specific religion.

CATHOLICISM AND MASONRY:

Can a Catholic become a Mason? There is nothing within of our doctrines which would prohibit a Catholic from becoming a Mason. There are many misunderstandings by the public, and by our own members, concerning this issue. These misunderstandings have led to many false conclusions, and created barriers where none exist, so far as Freemasonry is concerned. In other eras, some Catholic Popes regarded Masonry with disfavor and have issued edicts which condemned Freemasonry and prohibited membership to all Catholics. In spite of this, many prominent Catholics have become Masons. Our organization generally has given no official recognition to these edicts. We have chosen to follow a course of "silence and circumspection" since the first of these edicts was issued, in 1738, by Pope Clement XII.

SUBJECTS NOT PROPER FOR DISCUSSION IN LODGE:

Religion and politics should not be addressed in Lodge, and there are very good reasons why these subjects should not be discussed. When we meet in a Lodge, we are all on a common level, and are not subject to the classes and distinctions of the outside world. Each Brother is entitled to his own beliefs and may follow his own convictions. Our objective is to unite men, not to divide them. These subjects create honest differences of opinion which might well cause friction between Brethren. There will also be subjects concerning the Lodge's business that should not be discussed. All deliberations should be kept within the bounds of propriety and everyone should show a tolerance for the opinion of the other. Every Master wants harmony in his Lodge; and, once a matter has been put to vote in the Lodge and a decision is made, the decision should be accepted by all members, regardless of how they voted. We try to teach every Mason to be a good citizen and to perform his civic duties. We do not try to keep anyone from expressing his opinion, or from serving his city, county, state, or nation, in an honorable manner. Anyone who serves in political office should not act politically as a Freemason. Nor use the name of Freemasonry, in exercising his political rights - such as showing affiliation with any Lodge in his campaign advertising.

QUALIFICATIONS OF A PETITIONER:

The qualifications to be a Mason are few. The person must be a man, have a belief in a Supreme Being, at least 21 years old (in California), free of any previous felonious criminal convictions and be of good moral character. Loyalty to one's country is an essential qualification in Freemasonry, and only those are acceptable who cheerfully render obedience to every lawful authority. Disloyalty in any form is abhorrent to a Freemason, and is regarded as a serious Masonic Offense.

PREPARATION FOR INITIATION:

While Freemasonry is not a religion, its ceremonies are of a serious nature, dignified in its presentation and impart teachings which, if properly understood, obligate a man to lead a better life. To get the greatest good from the ceremonies, a candidate should first prepare his mind to understand and absorb these teachings. The

candidate should pay strict attention to every part of the ceremony, in order that he may gain some understanding of the teachings of Freemasonry. The methods we use in teaching will be new and unusual to the candidate. These methods have been used for over two centuries and have not changed significantly since they originated. Finally, he should learn that every Mason in the Lodge room is his friend and brother.

NO HORSEPLAY OR HAZING:

There is no place for horseplay or hazing during our ceremonies, and the candidate can be assured that there will be none. The rituals are serious and solemn, and we try to teach moral lessons with great dignity. Anything which is told to the candidate in a joking manner serves only to desecrate the honorable purposes of Freemasonry. The candidate should have no apprehension about entering a Lodge. He is always entering a society of friends and Brothers, where he will be treated with dignity and decorum at all times.

THE HEART OF THE MASONIC FAMILY:

Freemasonry is not just another fraternity or association of men banded together for social, political or economic advantages. Our foundation is built on a philosophy of friendship and brotherly love. We also make many worthwhile contributions to our society and community. For example, the California Grand Lodge manages two magnificent total care homes in Union City and Covina for our aged Brethren and their mothers, daughters, sisters and widows. In addition, the Masonic Home in Covina, cares for the disadvantaged children or Grandchildren of our membership.

FAMOUS FREEMASONS:

Many men whose names have been instrumental to the history and development of our civilization have been Freemasons. For your specific information, the following are but a few of the many famous historical figures that have engaged in our ceremonies.

EXPLORERS:

Hiram Bingham (Discoverer of Machu Picchu)
Adm. Richard E. Byrd

Christopher "Kit" Carson William Clark
Merriwether Lewis Robert E. Peary.

WORLD LEADERS:

Emilio Aguinaldo (Philippine Patriot and General)
Miguel Aleman (Mexican President 1947-52)
Edward Benes (President of Czechoslovakia 1939-48)
Sveinn Bjornsson (1st President of Iceland)
Simon Bolivar (George Washington of S. America)
Napoleon Bonaparte (and his four brothers)
King Charles XIII (King of Sweden 1748-1818)
King Edward VII,VIII (Kings of England)
Francis I, II (Holy Roman Emperors)
Frederick the Great (King of Prussia 1740-86)
George I & George II (Kings of Greece)
George IV & George VI (Kings of England)
Gustavus VI Adolphus (King of Sweden 1792-1809)
Kamehemeha IV, V (Kings of Hawaii)
Leopold I (King of Belgium (1831-65)
Peter the Great (Emperor of Russia 1689-1725)
William I (King of Prussia 186188)
William II (King of the Netherlands (1791849)
William IV (King of England (1830-37)

UNITED STATES PRESIDENTS:

George Washington
James Monroe
Andrew Jackson
James Polk
James Buchanan

Andrew Johnson

James Garfield William McKinley

Theodore Roosevelt

William H. Taft

Warren G. Harding

Franklin D. Roosevelt

Harry S. Truman

Gerald Ford

RELIGIOUS LEADERS:

James C. Baker (Bishop, Methodist Church, organized first Wesley Foundation in U.S.)

Hosea Ballou (Founder, Universalist Church)

Robert E. B. Baylor (Baptist clergyman, founder of Baylor University)

Preston Bradley (founder of the Peoples Church)

Father Francisco Calvo (Catholic Priest who started Freemasonry in Costa Rica in 1865)

Hugh I. Evans (National head of the Presbyterian Church, U.S.A.)

Most Reverend Geoffrey F. Fisher (former Archbishop of Canterbury)

Eugene M. Frank (Methodist Bishop)

Reverend Dr. Norman Vincent Peale (Methodist Episcopal minister and author)

Titus Low (President of Methodist Council of Bishops)

ENTERTAINMENT:

John Wayne

Gene Autry

Ernest Borgnine Joe E. Brown

Bob Burns

Eddie Cantor Charles D. Coburn

William F."Buffalo Bill" Cody Donald Crisp Cecil B. DeMille
Richard Dix
Douglas Fairbanks Sr. W.C. Fields
Clark Gable
Arthur Godfrey David W. Griffith
Oliver Hardy
Jean Hersholt Harry Houdini
Al Jolson
Charles "Buck" Jones Harry Kellar
Harold C. Lloyd
Tom Mix Dick Powell Will Rogers
Charles S. "Tom Thumb" Stratton Richard B. "Red" Skelton
Paul Whiteman
Ed Wynn Darryl Zanuck

UNITED STATES PATRIOTS:

Francis Scott Key (wrote our National Anthem)
Ralph Bellamy (wrote our Pledge of Allegiance)
Paul Revere
John Paul Jones
Benjamin Franklin
John Hancock
Patrick Henry

MILITARY LEADERS:

Generals John J. Pershing
George Marshall,
Douglas MacArthur
Joseph Stillwell
Johnathon Wainwright

Curtis E. LaMay

Omar N. Bradley

Henry H. "Hap" Arnold

Claire L. Chenault

Mark Clark

James Doolittle

Admirals David G. Farragut

Ernest J. King

Richard Byrd

SPORTS:

Grover C. Alexander

Cy Young

Jack Dempsey

Arnold Palmer

Tyrus R. "Ty" Cobb

Carl O. Hubbell

Christopher "Christy" Mathewson

Mordecai P.C. Brown

Gordon "Mickey" Corchran

Avery Brundage

Albert "Happy" Chandler

Branch Rickey

Knute Rockne

POLITICAL:

Sir Winston Churchill

Randolph Churchill

Thomas Dewey

Everett Dirksen

A. KEITH JONES

Fiorello H. LaGuardia
John Marshall
Barry Goldwater
Hubert Humphrey

COMPOSERS:

Irving Berlin
George M. Cohan
Wolfgang Amadeus Mozart
John Phillip Souza
Richard Wagner
Franz Joseph Haydn
Franz Listz

INVENTORS AND SCIENTISTS:

Samuel Colt (firearms)
Sir Alexander Fleming (penicillin)
Edward Jenner (vaccination)
Simon Lake (first practical submarine)
John L. McAdam (Macadamized roads)

YOUTH ORGANIZATION FOUNDERS:

Daniel Carter Beard (Boy Scouts)
Frank S. Land (International Order of DeMolay)
William Mark Sexton (International Order of Rainbow for Girls)

WRITERS:

Robert Burns
Samuel L. Clemens (Mark Twain)
Sir Arthur Conan Doyle (Sherlock Holmes)

Edward Gibbon (Decline and Fall of the Roman Empire),
Edgar A. Guest
Rudyard Kipling
Alexander Pope
Sir Walter Scott
Johathan Swift
Lowell Thomas
Voltair

SCULPTORS:

Gutzon Borglum and his son, Lincoln Borglum (carved Mt. Rushmore
National Memorial)
Johann G. Schadow (Prussian Court Sculptor)
J. Otto Schweizer

BUSINESS:

John Jacob Astor (financier)
Lloyd Balfour (Jewelry)
Lawrence Bell (Bell Aircraft Corp.)
William H. Dow (Dow Chemical Co.)
Henry Ford
Alfred Fuller (Fuller Brush)
King C. Gillett (Gillett Razor Co.)
Sir Thomas Lipton (tea)
Fredrick Maytag
Andrew W. Mellon (banker)
James C. Penny
George Pullman
David Sarnoff (father of T.V.)
Leland Stanford (railroads - Stanford Univ.)

ASTRONAUTS:

Ed Aldrin

Neil Armstrong

Gordon Cooper Don Eisle

Virgil Grissom

Ed Michell Tom Stafford

Fred Haise,

Wally Shirra.

NOTABLE AFRICAN AMERICAN MASONS

*Thurgood Marshall (Associate Justice, U.S. Supreme Court)

* Alex Haley (author)

* Booker T. Washington (educator/founder Tuskegee Institute)

* Charles B. Rangel (U.S. Congressman New York)

* Louis Stokes (U.S. Congressman Ohio)

* William "Count" Basie (orchestra leader/composer)

* Nathaniel "Nat King" Cole (American pianist and singer)

* W.E.B. DuBois (educator/author/historian)

* Edward Kennedy "Duke" Ellington (orchestra leader/composer)

 Medger Wiley Evers (civil rights leader)

James Herbert "Eubie" Blake (composer/pianist)

Andrew Young, (former mayor of Atlanta)

Thomas Bradley (mayor of Los Angeles, California)

Sugar Ray Robinson (mid/light heavy boxing champion)

John H. Johnson (publisher EBONY and Jet magazines)

Carl B. Stokes (first Black elected mayor, Cleveland, OH)

Robert Sengstacke Abbott (founder/publisher CHICAGO) DEFENDER

Richard Allen (founder/first bishop AME Church)

Matthew Henson (explorer)

Daniel "Chappie" James (general U.S. Air Force)

James Forten (abolitionist/manufacturer)

Timothy Thomas Fortune (journalist) Richard D. Gidron, president (Dick Gidron Cadillac)

William C. Handy (composer)

Augustus F. Hawkins (U.S. Congressman California)

Lionel Hampton (orchestra leader/composer)

Benjamin L. Hooks (Former Executive Director NAACP)

Benjamin Mays (educator/former president Atlanta University)

Ralph H. Metcalfe (Olympic champion)

A. Phillip Randolph (founder/ first president, International Brotherhood of Sleeping Car Porters)

Egbert Austin "Bert" Williams (actor/ comedian)

Harry A. Williamson (author/Masonic historian)

Scottie Pippen, #33 (Chicago Bulls / Forward)

CHAPTER 2

Masonic Government

And

Jurisprudence

"Setting the Rules"

INTRODUCTION TO MASONIC STRUCTURAL ORGANIZATION

The Grand Lodge

There are many different jurisdictions of governance of Freemasonry, each sovereign and independent of the other, and usually defined according to a geographic territory. Thus there is no central Masonic authority, although each jurisdiction maintains a list of other jurisdictions that it formally *recognizes*. If the other jurisdiction reciprocates the recognition, the two jurisdictions are said to be *in amity*, which permits the members of the one jurisdiction to attend closed meetings of the other jurisdiction's Lodges, and vice-versa. Generally speaking, to be recognized by another jurisdiction, one must (at least) meet that jurisdiction's requirements for *regularity*. This generally means that one must have in place, at least, the *ancient landmarks* of Freemasonry—the essential characteristics considered to be universal to Freemasonry in any culture. In keeping with the decentralized and non-dogmatic nature of Freemasonry, however, there is no universally accepted list of landmarks, and even jurisdictions in amity with each other often have completely different ideas as to what those landmarks are. Many jurisdictions take no official position at all as to what the landmarks are.

Freemasonry is often said to consist of two different branches: the Anglo and the Continental traditions. In reality, there is no tidy way to split jurisdictions into distinct camps like this. For instance, jurisdiction A might recognize B, which recognizes C, which does not recognize A. In addition, the geographical territory of one jurisdiction may overlap with another's, which may affect their relations, for purely territorial reasons. In other cases, one jurisdiction may overlook irregularities in another due simply to a desire to maintain friendly relations. Also, a jurisdiction may be formally affiliated with one tradition, while maintaining informal ties with the other. For all these reasons, labels like "Anglo" and "Continental" must be taken only as rough indicators, not as any kind of clear designation.

CONCORDANT BODIES

Freemasonry is associated with several *appendant bodies*, such as the Scottish Rite, which is a system of Freemasonry governed by an authority known as the United Supreme Council of The Ancient Accepted Scottish Rite for the Thirty-Third and Last Degree of Free Masonry. They represent the Northern and Southern Jurisdiction in which they are defined geographically.

The York Rite which includes three sovereign and distinct rites: the Holy Royal Arch, Royal and Select Masters (Cryptic Masonry), and Knights Templar. In regard to the (Masonic) Templars, this particular organization is limited to Cryptic Masons of the Christian faith and does not in any way impose this requirement on the entire York Rite system, as is commonly and erroneously believed.

Another group include the Ancient Egyptian Arabic Order of the Nobles of the Mystic Shrine (Shriners), which tend to expand on the teachings of Craft or Blue Lodge Masonry, while improving their members and society as a whole. The Shrine tend to emphasise fun and philanthropy and are largely a North American phenomenon. To all of these descriptive organization, North American Masonry has made run for the inclusion to its ranks Women Auxillaries, most prominent of these is the Order of Eastern Star, which is the foundation for all women auxillaries.

Different jurisdictions vary in how they define their relationship with such bodies, if at all. Some may give them some sort of formal recognition, while others may consider them wholly outside of Freemasonry proper. Not all such bodies will be universally considered as *appendant bodies*, some being simply considered as more or less separate organizations that happen to require Masonic affiliation for membership. Some of these organizations may have additional religious requirements, compared to Freemasonry proper (or "Craft Masonry"), since they approach Masonic teachings from a particular perspective.

There are also certain youth organizations (mainly North American) which are associated with Freemasonry, but are not necessarily Masonic in their content, such as the Knights of Phythagoras and the Order of DeMolay for boys and the International Order of the Rainbow for girls who have Masonic sponsorship.

THE CHARGES OF FREEMASONRY

General

ANCIENT CHARGES; The Charges of a Freemason, as they were collected from the old records of the Fraternity, under the superintendence of Bro. Jas Anderson, and the learned committee who acted with him, and given to the craft, through, in 1723, by order of the GRAND LODGE of England, in 1721, have been, wherever promulgated, accepted and acknowledged as containing the essence of the fundamental *Principles and Laws of Masonry.*

I.   Of GOD and Religion

II. Of the Civil Magistrate, supreme and subordinate

III. Of Lodge

IV. Of Masters, Wardens, Fellows and Apprentices

V.   Of the Management of the Craft in working

VI. Of Behavior

    1. In the Lodge while constituted.

    2. After the Lodge is over and the Brethren not gone.

    3. When Brethren meet without strangers, but not in a Lodge.

4. In presence of strangers not masons.

5. At Home and in the neighborhood.

6. Toward a strange Brother.

CONCERNING GOD AND RELIGION

A mason is obliged by his Tenure, to obey the moral law; and if he rightly understands the Art, he will never be a stupid Atheist nor an irreligious Libertine. But though in ancient times Masons were charged in every Country to be of the Religion of that Country or Nation, whatever it was, yet 'tis now though more expedient only to oblige them to that Religion in which all men agree, leaving their particular opinion to themselves; that is, to be good and true Men, or men of Honor and Honesty, by whatever Denomination or persuasion they may be distinguished; whereby Masonry become the Center of Union, and the Means of conciliating true friendship among Persons that must have remained at a perpetual Distance.

I. OF the CIVIL MASGISTRATES, supreme and subordinate

A Mason is a peaceable Subject to the Civil Powers, wherever he resides or works, and is never to be concerned in plots and conspiracies against Peace and Welfare of the Nation, nor to behave himself undutiful to interior Magistrates; for as Masonry hath been always injured by War, Bloodshed and Confusion, so ancient Kings and Princes have been much disposed to encourage the Craftsmen, because of their peaceableness and Loyalty, whereby they practically answered the Cavils of their adversaries, and promoted the Honor of the Fraternity, who ever flourished in Time of Peace. So that if a Brother should be Rebel against the State he is not to be countenanced in his rebellion, however he may be pitied as any unhappy Man; and, if convicted of no other Crime though the Loyal Brotherhood must and ought to disown his rebellion, and give no umbrage or ground of political jealousy to the Government for the time being, they cannot expel him from the LODGE, and his Relation to it remains indefeasible.

II. Of LODGES

A LODGE is a place where Masons assemble and work; Hence that Assembly, or duly organized Society of Masons, is called a LODGE, and every Brother ought to belong to one, and to be subject to its By-Laws and the General Regulations. It is either particular or general, and be best understood by attending it, and by the Regulations of the General or GRAND LODGE hereunto annexed. In ancient Times, no Mason or Fellow could be absent from it especially when warned to appear at it, without incurring a severe censure, until it appeared to the Master and Wardens the pure Necessity hindered him. The persons admitted Members of a LODGE must be good and true Men, freeborn, and of mature and discreet Age, no Bondmen, no Women, no immoral or scandalous men shall be admitted, but only those of good report.

III. OF MASTERS, WARDENS, FELLOWS and APPRENTICES

All preferment among Masons is grouped upon real Worth and personal Merit only, that so the LORDS may be well served, the Brethren not put to shame, nor the Royal Craft despised: therefore no Master or Warden is chosen by Seniority, but for his Merit. It is impossible to describe these things in writing, and every Brother must attend in his place, and learn them in a way peculiar to this Fraternity: Only Candidates may know that no Master should take an Apprentice unless he has Sufficient Employment for him, and unless he be a perfect youth having no maim of defects in his body that may render him incapable of learning the Art of serving his Master's LORD, and of being made a Brother, and then a Fellow-Craft in due time, even after he has served such a term of years as the customs of the Country directs; and that he should be descended of Honest Parents; that so, when otherwise qualified he may arrive to the Honor of being the Warden, and then the Master of the LODGE, the Grand Warden, and at length the Grand Master of all the LODGES, according to his Merit. No Brother can be a Warden until he has passed the part of a Fellow-Craft; nor a Master until he has acted as a Warden, nor Grand Warden until he has been Master of a LODGE, nor Grand Master unless he has been a Fellow Craft before his Election, who is also to be nobly born, or a Gentleman of the best Fashion, or some eminent Scholar, or some curious Architect, or Artist, descended of Honest Parents, and who is of similar great Merit in the opinion of the LODGES. These Rulers and Governors, supreme and subordinate, of the ancient LODGE, are to be obeyed in their respective Stations by all the Brethren, according to the old Charges and Regulations, with all Humility, Reverence, Love and Alacrity.

IV. OF MANAGEMENT of the CRAFT in WORKING

All Masons shall work honestly on Working days, that they may live creditably on Holy Days; and the time appointed by the Laws of the Land or confirmed by Custom shall be observed. The most expert of the Fellow-Craftsmen shall be chosen or appointed the Master or Overseer of the Lord's Work; who is to be called Master by those that work under him. The Craftsmen are to avoid all ill Language, and to call each other by no disobliging Name, but Brother or Fellow; and to behave themselves courteously within and without the Lodge.

The Master, knowing himself to be able of Cunning, shall undertake the Lord's Work as reasonably as possible, and truly dispend his Goods as if they were his own; nor to give more Wages to any Brother or Apprentice than he really may deserve. Both the Master and the Masons receiving their Wages justly, shall be faithful to the Lord and honestly finish their Work, whether Task or journey; nor put the work to Task that hath been accustomed to Journey. None shall discover Envy at the Prosperity of a Brother, nor supplant him, or put him out of his Work, if he be capable to finish the same; for no man can finish another's Work so much to the Lord's Profit, unless he be thoroughly acquainted with the Designs and Draughts of him that began it. When a Fellow-Craftsman is chosen Warden of the Work under the Master, he shall be true both to Master and Fellows, shall carefully oversee the Work in the Master's Absence to the Lord's profit; and his Brethren shall obey him. All Masons employed shall meekly receive their Wages without Murmuring or Mutiny, and not desert the Master till the Work is finished. A younger Brother shall be instructed in working, to prevent spoiling the Materials for want of Judgment, and for increasing and continuing of brotherly love. All the Tools used in working shall be approved by the Grand Lodge. No Laborer shall be employed in the proper Work of Masonry; nor shall Free Masons work with those that are not free, without an urgent Necessity; nor shall they teach Laborers and unaccepted Masons as they should teach a Brother or Fellow.

VI. Of BEHAVIOUR.

I. In the LODGE while CONSTITUTED.

You are not to hold private Committees, or separate Conversation without Leave from the Master, nor to talk of anything impertinent or unseemly, nor interrupt the Master or Wardens, or any Brother speaking to the Master: Nor behave yourself ludicrously or jestingly while the Lodge is engaged in what is serious and solemn; nor use any unbecoming Language upon any Pretense whatsoever; but to pay due Reverence to your Master, Wardens, and Fellows, and put them to Worship. If any Complaint be brought, the Brother found guilty shall stand to the Award and Determination of the Lodge, who are the proper and competent Judges of all such Controversies (unless you carry it by Appeal to the Grand Lodge), and to whom they ought to be referred, unless a Lord's Work be hindered the meanwhile, in which Case a particular Reference may be made; but you must never go to Law about what concern Masonry, without an absolute necessity apparent to the Lodge.

2. BEHAVIOUR after the LODGE is over and the BRETHREN not GONE

You may enjoy yourself with innocent Mirth, treating one another according to Ability, but avoiding all Excess, or forcing any Brother to eat or drink beyond his Inclination, or hindering him from going when his Occasions call him, or doing or saying anything offensive, or that may forbid an easy and free Conversation, for that would blast our Harmony, and defeat our laudable Purposes. Therefore no private Piques or Quarrels must be brought within the Door of the Lodge, far less any Quarrels about Religion, or Nations, or State Policy, we being only, as Masons, of the Universal Religion above mentioned, we are also of all Nations, Tongues, Kindreds, and Languages, and are resolved against all Politics, as what never yet conducted to the Welfare of the Lodge, nor ever will.

3. BEHAVIOUR when BRETHREN meet WITHOUT STRANGERS, but not in a LODGE Formed.

You are to salute one another in a courteous Manner, as you will be instructed, calling each other Brother, freely giving mutual instruction as shall be thought expedient, without being ever seen or overheard, and without encroaching upon each other, or derogating from that Respect which is due to any Brother, were he not Mason: For though all Masons are as Brethren upon the same Level, yet Masonry takes no Honor from a man that he had before; nay, rather it adds to his Honor, especially if he has deserve well of the Brotherhood, who must give Honor to whom it is due, and avoid ill Manners.

4. BEHAVIOUR in presence of Strangers NOT MASONS.

You shall be cautious in your Words and Carriage, that the most penetrating Stranger shall not be able to discover or find out what is not proper to be intimated, and sometimes you shall divert a Discourse, and manage it prudently for the Honor of the worshipful Fraternity.

5. BEHAVIOUR at HOME, and in Your NEIGHBORHOOD

You are to act as becomes a moral and wise Man; particularly not to let your Family, Friends and Neighbors know the Concern of the Lodge, &c., but wisely to consult your own Honor, and that of the ancient Brotherhood, for reasons not to be mentioned here You must also consult your Health, by not continuing together too late, or too long from Home, after Lodge Hours are past; and by avoiding of Gluttony or Drunkenness, that your Families be not neglected or injured, nor you disabled from working.

6. BEHAVIOUR toward a Strange BROTHER.

You are cautiously to examine him, in such a Method as Prudence shall direct you, that you may not be imposed upon by an ignorant, false Pretender, ...whom you are to reject with contempt and Derision, and beware of giving him any Hints of Knowledge.

But if you discover him to be a true and genuine Brother, you are to respect him accordingly; and if he is in Want, you must relieve him if you can, or else direct him how he may be relieved; you must employ him some days, or else recommend him to be employed. But you are not charged to do beyond your ability, only to prefer a poor Brother, that is a good Man and true before any other poor People in the same Circumstance. Finally, All these Charges you are to observe, and also those that shall be recommended to you in another Way; cultivating Brotherly Love, the Foundation and Cap-stone, the Cement and Glory of this Ancient Fraternity, avoiding all wrangling and quarreling, all Slander and Backbiting, nor permitting others to slander any honest Brother, but defending his Character, and doing him all good Offices, as far as is consistent with your Honor and Safety, and no farther. And if any of them do you Injury you must apply to your own or his Lodge, and from thence you may appeal to the Grand Lodge, at the Quarterly Communication and from thence to the annual Grand Lodge, as has been the ancient laudable Conduct but when the Case cannot be otherwise decided, and patiently listening to the honest and friendly Advice of Master and Fellows when they would prevent your going to Law with Strangers, or would excite you to put a speedy Period to all Lawsuits, so that you may mind the Affair of Masonry with the more Alacrity and Success; but with respect to Brothers or Fellows at Law, the Master and Brethren should kindly offer their Mediation, which ought to be thankfully submitted to by the contending Brethren; and if that submission is impracticable, they must, however, carry on their Process, or Lawsuit, without Wrath and Rancor (not In the common way) saying or doing nothing which may hinder Brotherly Love, and good Offices to be renewed and continued; that all may see the benign Influence of Masonry, as all true Masons have done from the beginning of the World, and will do to the End of Time.

MASONIC GOVERNMENT

In the beginning of this examination we hasten to assure the reader that we do not propose to bring forward the testimony of non-Masons or of anti-Masonic publications. We do not propose to beg the question in any way, manner or shape, and if the reader should have been so unfortunate as to have ever been made a Freemason, we ask and hope that for the time being he will forget that fact, and having divested his mind if possible, of prejudice, will look at the subject from a common sense standpoint, neither accepting; nor rejecting a point or proposition until all the bearings are duly weighed. You are not responsible for the present form, character and government of Freemason, neither is the writer. because we had nothing whatever to do in originating, molding or shaping the system. However, we do have a right to look at the facts in the case, intelligently draw our conclusions there from and then to "mark and govern ourselves accordingly," no man or set of men daring to lawfully molest us or make us afraid.

Now it is plain to every one that if anybody really knows what Freemasonry is, Freemasons themselves certainly must know; and if any Masons know, it is not necessarily the embryo, three-degree, pinfeather, Blue Lodge Masons, who perhaps do not know enough to visit a strange lodge without a brother along to vouch for them, but it is self-evident that if any Masons know what the principles, doctrines and practice of the order are, it is the men who have gone from the "ground floor" clear through the "pictures." who have made Freemasonry a life study, who are even now occupying the highest positions of honor and power in the craft, and who have been put forward by the institution to write its great standard publications including its rituals, its monitors, its manuals, its lexicons, its dictionaries, its digests of Masonic law, together with its works on Masonic jurisprudence, its histories, its guides, its trestle-boards, and many other valuable works issued for the sole benefit of the "Worshipful Fraternity."

The great Masonic works and documents herein quoted were written by the learned rulers and teachers of Masonry and are protected by the seal of the United States in copyright. They were written by high Masons, copyrighted by Masons, published by Masons, sold by Masons, sold to Masons and openly endorsed and used by the Masonic Fraternity all over this land. Not only endorsed and used by well posted individual Masons, but subordinate and Grand Lodges have officially fathered and are using them. With this understanding, reader, we will meet upon the " level " and part upon the "square." First we will secure the evidence and testimony, and by and by determine the real Masonic character and exact standing of the numerous witnesses.

THE GOVERNMENT OF THE FRATERNITY.

" The mode of Government observed by the fraternity will give the best idea of the nature and design of the Masonic institution." *Sickels' Freemasons' Monitor, p. 10.*

Very well; it is the BEST explanation that we are after and so we will examine into Masonic Government.

SYNOPSIS OF MASONIC LAW.

"The system of Masonic law has little of the republican or democratic spirit about It."—*Rob Morris, in Webb's Freemasons' Monitor, revised edition, p. 195*

Well that is not very encouraging to patriotic men but perhaps all will be satisfactorily explained as we progress.

"We may not call in question the propriety of this organization; if we would be Masons we must *yield private judgment.* 'To the law and to the testimony—if any man walk not by this rule it is because there is no light in him.'"—*Pierson's Traditions of Freemasonry, p. 30.*

That certainly is not republicanism or democracy, because they are inclined to give a man increased liberty and privileges instead of calling for the surrender thereof. But let us see how far this surrender of personal liberty is demanded of the Mason.

"That this surrender of free-will to Masonic authority is *absolute* (within the scope of the landmarks Of the order) and *perpetual,* may be inferred from an examination of the emblem (the shoe or sandal) which is used to enforce this lesson of resignation. The esotery of the Masonic rituals gives the fullest assurance of this: "once a Mason always a Mason" is an aphorism in our literature conveying an undeniable truth."—*Morris' Dictionary, p. 29.*

Then the surrender of personal private judgment and freewill to Freemasonry is complete and binding for all time. Well said indeed; for surely that is anything except Americanism, as either republicanism or democracy.

"A Mason should know how to obey those who are set over him, however inferior they may be in worldly rank; or condition." —*Macoy's Masonic Monitor, p. 14.*

What is this authority set over the Freemason to which he has bound himself and what will be the result of disobedience?

Disobedience and want of respect to Masonic superiors is an offense for which the transgressor subjects himself to punishment."—*Mackey's Masonic Jurisprudence , p. 511.*

Superiors and inferiors—queer government that—Americans are all equals. How severely will an offender be punished?

DISOBEDIENCE

"Under the head of Discipline is given a catalogue of fifteen prime classes of un-Masonic acts, of which this is one. It is so subversive of the groundwork of Masonry, in which obedience is most strongly inculcated, that the Mason who disobeys subjects himself to severe penalties."— *Morris' Dictionary of Freemasonry, pp. 91,92*

This no doubt was the punishment meted out to William Morgan and many ,others for their disobedience. Who Is the representative of Freemasonry, wielding such extraordinary authority?

"As a presiding officer the Master is possessed or extra-ordinary powers which belong to the presiding officer of no other association" *Mackey's Masonic Jurisprudence, p. 344.*

Indeed! His Majesty must be quite a privileged character, having such wonderful powers that are possessed by no other presiding officer.

"The powers and privileges of' the Master of a lodge are by no means limited in extent."—*Chase's Digest of Masonic Law, page 380.*

Not limited means unlimited, and that is just about as much as an ordinary mortal can well comprehend.

"The power of a Master in his lodge is absolute."— *Mackey's Lexicon of Freemasonry, p. 296.*

There it is, a system of absolute masters; and an absolute master cannot exist without abject slavery; one is necessary to the other, so who are the miserable Masonic slaves? Let the reader answer that all important question.

"Hence, we find that the Master's authority in the lodge is despotic as the Sun ~n the firmament, which was placed there by the Creator, never to deviate from its accustomed course. till the declaration is 'promulgated that time shall be no more." *Oliver's Signs and & Symbols of Freemasonry, p. 142.*

Where, in all the annals of history, ancient or modern, describing all the monarchies, despotisms and tyrannies from the dawn of creation down to the present time, will you find a better description of an irresponsible, absolute despot, than the above synopsis of the power of the Master of a subordinate)Masonic lodge" *To* whom, or to what, is this Masonic nabob beholden ?

"The Master is responsible for his official acts, not to his lodge, but to the Grand Lodge: or (which is the same thing) to the Grand Master for the time being."—*Webb's Freemasons' Monitor, p. 271.*

What is the nature and power of the Grand Lodge is the next question staring us in the face for adjustment.

GRAND LODGES—JURISDICTION OF.

"A Grand Lodge is invested with power and authority over all the craft within its jurisdiction. It is the Supreme Court of Appeal in all Masonic cases, and to its decrees unlimited obedience must be paid by every lodge and every Mason situated within its control. The government of Grand Lodges is, therefore, completely despotic. While a Grand Lodge exists, its edicts must be respected and obeyed without examination by its subordinate lodges." —*Mackey's Lexicon of Freemasonry, p. 186.*

The Grand Lodge being completely despotic, therefore the Worshipful Master of a subordinate lodge is as much a slave to it as are the poor deceived and deluded victims over whom he lords it with such pomposity. But suppose, as is often the case, that some conscientious man who has been inveigled into the order should object and rebel against some mandate or edict of the Grand Lodge that he is fully convinced and persuaded is not right and proper; Will he be coerced into a compliance therewith ?

"The first duty of the reader of this Synopsis is to obey the edicts of his Grand Lodge. Right or wrong, his very existence as a Mason hangs upon obedience to the powers immediately set above him. Failure in this must infallibly bring down expulsion, which, as a Masonic death, ends all The one unpardonable crime in a Mason *is contumacy,* or disobedience."— *Webb's Freemasons' Monitor, p. 196.*

What is the one unpardonable crime in a Freemason? Is it lying, stealing, murder or a violation of civil law? Nay, verily, but it is simply to disobey *Masonic* law. That law must be obeyed, right or wrong. Does this low down slavery run through every department of Freemasonry, or only in the Blue Lodge and not In the higher grades?

"The principle of submission and obedience runs through the whole system and constitutes one of the greatest safeguards of our institution. The Mason is obedient to the Master, the Master and Lodge to the Grand Lodge, and this in its turn to the old landmarks and ancient regulations of the order. Thus is a due degree of subordination kept up and the institution preserved in its primitive purity."—*Pierson's Traditions of' Freemasonry, p. 30.*

This is a most galling system of human slavery a hundred-fold more degrading than ever was African bondage in that both soul and body are the property of Freemasonry leaving the individual member a mere machine in the hands of Masonic superiors. Do Masons, deep down in their souls endorse and revere such a vile system as Freemasonry.

PREPARATION—BLUE LODGE MASONRY.

"If any applicant is not prepared in his heart he will never make a Mason no matter what dramatic exercises he may be put through. or what discipline exerted upon him."—*Morris' Dictionary of Freemasonry, pp. 243, 244.*

What is it that binds a man to this "Invisible Empire" or to this secret despotism? We go to the above named Masonic dictionary for " more light."

COVENANT BLUE LODGE MASONRY.

" The obligations of Masonry are, in the sense of the definition, covenants and so are the Constitution and By-laws."—*Ibid., P. 76.*

The obligations, then, along with the bylaws and constitution are covenants and we will now see what it is that makes a Mason.

OBLIGATION

"It is 'the Obligation which makes the Mason' and the difference between one Mason and another consists simply in the fact that one keeps his obligations better than another."—*Morris' Dictionary of Freemasonry, p. 218.*

That is the nature and form of the Masonic obligation. Is it simply a promise or affirmation or is it construed to be an oath with all the binding force of the same? Turning again to our friendly dictionary we learn this:

AFFIRMAT10N—BLUE LODGE MASONRY.

"An affirmation is not equivalent to an oath in Masonry however it may be in common and is not legitimate in the working of the lodge."—*Ibid. p.13.*

Now, sir does Freemasonry consider and teach its devotees to consider the so-called Masonic oath equal or superior in binding force to the civil oath?

COVENANTS.

"The Covenant is irrevocable. Even though a person may be suspended or expelled; though he may withdraw from the Lodge, journey into countries where Masons cannot be found, or become a subject of despotic governments that persecute, or a communicant of bigoted churches that denounce Masonry, he cannot cast off or nullify his Masonic covenant; No law of the land can affect it—no anathema of the church weaken it. It is irrevocable." —*Webb's Freemasons' Monitor, p. 240.*

This accounts for many strange and mysterious proceedings in our would-be courts of justice and in the churches. NO law of the land (that is, civil law,) can even affect this lodge oath or covenant. No anathema of the church (that is, divine law), can so much as weaken it. Is it any wonder that criminals go scot-free when the sheriff that impanels the jury, enough of the jurors impaneled to bring in a divided verdict, enough witnesses drummed up to make the evidence appear contradictory, the attorneys of the prosecution and of the defense, and the judge on the bench, are irrevocably bound to the prisoner at the bar as sworn brethren, by an obligation considered paramount to all others, civil or divine?

Is it anything strange that there is trouble in the church when the members are bound up, by this strong covenant, with saloon-keepers, irreverent scoffers, and other evil-minded men, in sworn brotherhood? Is there no escape from Masonic thralldom? is the now all important question.

"No method is provided for in the Masonic jurisprudence of modern times by which a member can withdraw himself from the authority of the society. He may resign his membership in the lodge, deny its government, even repudiate the ties by which he is bound to the institution, yet that authority remains unbroken. A 'due summons' from the Lodge or Grand lodge is obligatory upon him; and should he refuse obedience he will be disgracefully expelled from the society with public marks of ignominy that can never be erased."—*Morris' Dictionary of Freemasonry, page 29.*

What arrogant system is this, that proposes to take a man's manhood from him by imposing upon him an obligation that defies both his civil as well as the divine law? It even declares vengeance on all who dare to think and act as free men without first consulting the Masonic covenant. No wonder seceded Masons and out-spoken non-Masons are abused, vilified, slandered and hounded down by Masonic minions. " Public marks of ignominy that can never be erased."

"The expulsion of a Mason, while it deprives him of every privilege with which his Masonic attachment endowed him, leaves him bound by every part and point of his. Masonic covenant. Of this no act of his own or of the lodge can ever divest him. The tie of Masonry is perpetual."— *Webb's Freemasons' Monitor, p. 257.*

That certainly is a queer government if there ever was one. The mystery of the whole business is to discover how under the sun a man can be a loyal citizen of any civil government on earth and at the same time uphold this system of secret despotism that boldly and openly defies all governments?

"There is no charge more frequently made against Freemasonry than that of its tendency to revolution and conspiracy, and to political organizations which may affect the peace of society, or interfere with the rights of government."—*Mackey's Mystic Tie of Freemasonry, p. S6.*

Well, does this great Masonic ruler and law-giver speak the truth in the above, for time and again different governments have been compelled to suppress Freemasonry because of its incompatibility with the peace of society and with the laws of the land in that it harbored criminals and perverted the equitable administration of civil law.

"There is no duty more forcibly enjoined in Masonry, than that of warning a brother of danger impending to his person or interests. To neglect this is a positive violation of obligation, and destroys any person's claim to be entitled a Mason:."— *Morris' Dictionary of Freemasonry, p. 25.*

Are Masons obliged to give this warning to affiliates only, or must they always warn and aid one another discriminately?

"We are to give aid in imminent peril when Masonically called upon, not lest injustice may be done if we pause to inquire into the question of affiliation, but because the obligation to give this aid, which is reciprocal among all Masons, never has been and never can be canceled."— *Mackey's Masonic Jurisprudence, p. 270.*

Shall the Mason pause to inquire as to ANYTHING
When Masonically appealed to for aid?

"If a person appeals to us as a Mason in imminent peril, or such pressing need that we have not time to inquire into his worthiness, then, lest we might refuse to relieve and aid a worthy brother' we must not stop to inquire as to anything."—*Albert Pike, in Masonic Grand Lodge Report of Arkansas;* Also *Mackey's Masonic Jurisprudence, p. -70.*

Ex-Confederate General Albert Pike who led a brigade of Indian savages against the flag of his country at the battle of Pea Ridge, Arkansas, where the dead and wounded boys in Blue were scalped! and tomahawked, and even mutilated in a manner too barbarous and obscene for description, by his followers, and whose rebel hands are dyed crimson by the blood of loyal American citizens, is now the most honored man in Freemasonry.

He has since been very appropriately placed at the pinnacle of the system, where he sits supreme ruler; and to him every Freemason, knowingly or unknowingly, yet, nevertheless truly, does honor and homage when he throws A due-guard and sign at a Blue Lodge Master; for the principle of submission and obedience runs through the WHOLE system," while in giving the sign he acknowledges himself to be under death-penalty to obey this Masonic superior. Such is Freemasonry, a hot-bed of disloyalty and treason, according to our deductions thus far.

"Treason and rebellion also, because they are altogether political offenses, cannot be inquired into by a lodge; and al. though a Mason may be convicted of either of these acts in the courts of his country, he cannot be Masonically punished; and not withstanding his treason or rebellion his relation to the lodge, to use the language of the old Charges, remains indefeasible."—*Mackey's Masonic Jurisprudence, p. 510 !*

This makes plain why perhaps the blackest-hearted rebel in the land is very appropriately placed at the head of treasonable Masonry in this country. Thus a saint in Freemasonry may be the worst citizen in this government.

"The Mason who is at home and the Mason who comes from abroad are considered on an equal footing as to all Masonic rights; and hence the brother made in Europe is as much a Mason when he comes to America, and is as fully qualified to discharge in America all Masonic functions, without any form of naturalization, as though he had been made in this country. The converse is equally true."— *Mackey's Masonic Jurisprudence, p. 200.*

What a remarkable array of Masonic testimony! and yet the half has not been told, as we might go on almost indefinitely showing the foul, treasonable and anti-republican nature, as legibly portrayed under the systematically arranged headings of the great copyrighted standard Masonic publications. The above Masonic quotations are complete sentences and not garbled. The language is so concise and plain that a child can easily analyze each sentence. The quotations are authoritative; Masonic superiors never argue Masonry with subordinates. And now we proceed to nail the above synopsis of Masonic law and government by home testimony.

We will let every affiliated Freemason in the Missouri Masonic Grand Lodge jurisdiction testify through their Grand Lodge Reports, three copies of which must be filed away year by year in every subordinate lodge throughout the jurisdiction.

The members of all subordinate lodges are fully represented in Grand Lodge by the superior officers of the several lodges, as they are delegates thereto, and no document emanates from any Masonic Grand Lodge without its endorsement and approval. We will call our neighbors, and see how cheerfully they accept or reject the testimony of the brightest men in the order:

"The conclusion of the report breathes such a pure air of Masonic truths that we incorporate it herewith. It says: 'Once a Mason always a Mason—once a Mason, everywhere a Mason. However independent either as individuals or as lodges, whether Grand or subordinate—and we are each and all truly free and uncontrolled by anything, save our ancient laws and constitution—yet no Mason can be a foreigner to another Mason. We are all equal citizens of one common government, having equal rights, equal privileges and equal duties; and in which government, thank God, the majority does not govern.

For our order in its very constitution, strikes at the root of that which is the very basis of popular government It proclaims and practices, not that the will of the masses is wise and good, and as such to be obeyed,—not that the majority shall govern .. . but that the law tit e., above mentioned "ancient law"1 shall govern. Our tenet is not only that no single man but that no body of men (however wise or numerous)' can change in any decree one single landmark of our ancient institution. Our law is strictly organic; it cannot be changed without being destroyed. You may take a man to pieces, and you may take a watch to pieces, but you can not alter his organs and put him together again as you do the timekeeper.

Masonry is the living man, and all other forms of government mere convenient machines made by clever mechanics, for regulating the affairs of state. Not only do we know no North, no South, no East and no West, but we know no government save our own. To every government save that of Masonry, and to each and all alike, we are foreigners; and this form of government is neither pontifical, autocratic, monarchial republican, democratic nor despotic; it is a government *per se,* and that government is Masonic.

We have nothing to do with forms of government, forms of religion or forms of social life. We are a nation of men only, bound to each other by Masonic ties as citizens of the world, and that world, the world of Masonry—brethren to each other all the world over, foreigners to all the world beside. The above is a Masonic address in a nutshell—it is the compressed essence of Masonic life."—*Grand Lodge Report for, 1867.*

How does that sound to a loyal American? Missouri Freemasons therein positively affirm that they are not controlled by ANYTHING save Masonic law; they THANK GOD that in their government the majority does NOT govern; that Freemasonry strikes at the very base of free government; that it proclaims and practices that the will of the MASSES should not be obeyed; that the United States is a mere convenient machine only: together with many other treasonable doctrines that the Missouri Masonic Grand Lodge emphatically declares are the compressed essence of Masonic life. Later reports all breathe the spirit of double-dyed treason.

We would gladly prolong this discussion, but we will briefly consult another Grand Lodge Report or two and rest the case.

"For ourselves, we deny as Masons that any civil government on earth has the right to divide or curtail Masonic jurisdiction when once established. It can only be done by competent Masonic authority, and in accordance with Masonic usage."— Grand Lodge Report.

Rebold's History of Freemasonry, p. 62, says: "The Freemason receives not the law, he gives It;" and a late Grand Lodge Report puts on the cap-sheaf by adding:

"In all this we must not forget that 'Masonry is a law unto itself.' Its Perpetuity is dependent upon the force of its own influences. It never demands affiliation with any other humanizing agencies."—*Grand Lodge Report of 1880.*

MASONIC AUTHORS QUOTED ABOVE

Thomas Smith Webb, whose Masonic title was King, or Grand King, was a learned Mason, the first standard Masonic American author; or, in other words, he is the father of Masonry in this country.

Albert Pike: 33rd degree Most Puissant Sovereign Grand Commander of the Masons of the United States, author of the "Statutes of Ancient and Accepted Rite," etc. He is the supreme ruler of American Masonry.

Albert G. Mackey, ILL. .: Past Grand Secretary and Grand Lecturer of the Grand Lodge of South Carolina; Past Grand High Priest of the Grand Chapter of South Carolina; Secretary General of the Supreme Council, 33d degree, for the Southern Jurisdiction of the Masons of the United States; Past General Grand High Priest of the General Grand Chapter of the Masons of the United States; author of A LEXICON OF FREEMASONRY, MANUAL OF THE LODGE, THE BOOK OF THE CHAPTER, MYSTIC TIE, THE RITUALIST, MASONIC JURISPRUDENCE, etc., the latter a work that is to Masons and Blue

Lodge Masters what the Revised Statutes are to a Justice of the Peace, or what Blackstone's Commentaries are to members of the bar.

Daniel Sickels: Past Master, Past High Priest, Knight Templar, Past Junior Grand Warden, 33d degree Secretary General of the Supreme Council for the Northern Jurisdiction of the Masons of the United States, author of a FREEMASON'S MONITOR, GENERAL AHIMAN REZON, OR FREEMASONS' GUIDE, etc.

A.T. C. Pierson: Past Grand High Priest, Grand Captain General of the Grand Encampment of the Masons of The United States of America, 33rd degree Sovereign Grand Inspector general; was for ten years Grand Master and is at present Grand Secretary of the Masonic Grand Lodge of Minnesota; author of TRADITIONS OF FREEMASONRY, etc.

Rob Morris, L.L.D.: Knight Templar, Past Grand Master of the Masonic Grand Lodge of Kentucky, Sovereign Grand Inspector General, author of CODE OF MASONIC LAW, compiler of the UNIVERSAL MASONIC LIBRARY and HIS DICTIONARY OF FREEMASONRY is to Masonry what Webster's Dictionary is to the English language it is the great definer of Masonic terms.

Robert Macoy: 33°, Past Master, Past Grand Secretary, Past Grand Recorder, Past Grand Commander, National Grand Secretary, author of A CYCLOPEDIA OF FREEMASONRY, MANUAL OF THE ORDER OF THE EASTERN STAR, MASONIC VOCAL MANUAL, and other works.

George Wingate Chase: A high Freemason, a prolific Masonic author, having compiled no less than eight valuable Masonic publications, one of which is the great book of decisions, CHASE'S DIGEST

OF MASONIC LAW, a book that bears about the same relation to subordinate Masonic Lodges that the decisions of our Supreme Courts bear to our Circuit and County Courts.

Emanuel Rebold, M.D.: Past Deputy of the Masonic Grand Orient of France and a learned Masonic writer.

Rev. George Oliver: D.D., of England: Past Deputy Grand Master for Lincolnshire, and author of about twelve noble Masonic publications.

The above forementioned scripts are extracted articles from other copyrighted standard Masonic publications. The high Masonic standing and character of the authors here mentioned is fully sustained by Grand Lodge documents reposing on the table before us as we invite these lines.

PRINCIPIA

The Authorities for Masonic Law.

The laws which govern the institution of Freemasonry are of two kinds, *unwritten* and *written,* and may in a manner be compared with the "lex non scripta," or common law, and the "lex seripta," or statute law of English and American jurists.

The "lex non scripta," or *unwritten law* of Freemasonry is derived from the traditions, usages and customs of the fraternity as they have existed from the remotest antiquity, and as they are universally admitted by the general consent of the members of the Order. In fact, we may apply to these unwritten laws of Masonry the definition given by Blackstone of the "leges non scriptæ" of the English constitution—that "their original institution and authority are not set down in writing, as acts of parliament are, but they receive their binding power, and the force of laws, by long and immemorial usage and by their universal reception throughout the kingdom." When, in the course of this work, I refer to these unwritten laws as authority upon any point, I shall do so under the appropriate designation of "ancient usage."

The "lex scripta," or written law of Masonry, is derived from a variety of sources, and was framed at different periods. The following documents I deem of sufficient authority to substantiate any principle, or to determine any disputed question in Masonic law.

1. The "Ancient Masonic charges, from a manuscript of the Lodge of Antiquity," and said to have been written in the reign of James II.

2. The regulations adopted at the General Assembly held in 1663, of which the Earl of St. Albans was Grand Master.

3. The interrogatories propounded to the Master of a lodge at the time of his installation, and which, from their universal adoption, without alteration, by the whole fraternity, are undoubtedly to be considered as a part of the fundamental law of Masonry.

4. "The Charges of a Freemason, extracted from the Ancient Records of Lodges beyond sea, and of those in England, Scotland, and Ireland, for the use of the Lodges in London," printed in the first edition of the Book of Constitutions of that work.

5. The thirty-nine "General Regulations," adopted "at the annual assembly and feast held at Stationers' hall on St. John the Baptist's day, 1721," and which were published in the first edition of the Book of Constitutions.

6. The subsequent regulations adopted at various annual communications by the Grand Lodge of England, up to the year 1769, and published

in different editions of the Book of Constitutions. These, although not of such paramount importance and universal acceptation as the Old Charges and the Thirty-nine Regulations, are, nevertheless, of great value as the means of settling many disputed questions, by showing what was the law and usage of the fraternity at the times in which they were adopted.

Soon after the publication of the edition of 1769 of the Book of Constitutions, the Grand Lodges of America began to separate from their English parent and to organize independent jurisdictions. From that period, the regulations adopted by the Grand Lodge of England ceased to have any binding efficacy over the craft in this country, while the laws passed by the American Grand Lodges lost the character of general regulations, and were invested only with local authority in their several jurisdictions. Before concluding this introductory section, it may be deemed necessary that something should be said of the "Ancient Landmarks of the Order," to which reference is so often made.

Various definitions have been given of the landmarks. Some suppose them to be constituted of all the rules and regulations which were in existence anterior to the revival of Masonry in 1717, and which were confirmed and adopted by the Grand Lodge of England at that time. Others, more stringent in their definition, restrict them to the modes of recognition in use among the fraternity. I am disposed to adopt a middle course, and to define the Landmarks of Masonry to be, all those usages and customs of the craft—whether ritual or legislative—whether they relate to forms and ceremonies, or to the organization of the society—which have existed from time immemorial, and the alteration or abolition of which would materially affect the distinctive character of the institution or destroy its identity. Thus, for example, among the legislative landmarks, I would enumerate the office of Grand Master as the presiding officer over the craft, and among the ritual landmarks, the legend of the third degree. But the laws, enacted from time to time by Grand Lodges for their local government, no matter how old they may be, do not constitute landmarks, and may, at any time, be altered or expunged, since the 39th regulation declares expressly that "every annual Grand Lodge has an inherent is ancient fraternity, provided always that the old landmarks carefully preserved.

Scope of Masonic Law

The actions of Freemasons, in their Grand or Subordinate Lodges, or in their Individual character, is regulated and controlled by;

1. Ancient Landmarks, or the unwritten Law of Masonry.

2. Written Constitutions and General Regulations, and...

3. Usages, Customs, Rules, Edicts and Resolutions, having the force as those of GENERAL REGULATIONS.

The **ANCIENT LANDMARKS** are those principles of Masonic Government and policy which are the only part of Masonic Law or Rules of Government that may not be altered or disturbed; as such for them to be written and are usually, but not wholly, engrafted in the written Constitution and General Regulation.

CONSTITUTIONS are those written compacts or Laws adopted by Freemasons for the Government of a Grand Lodge and its Subordinate Lodges and their members, including General Regulations, constitutionally, that are intended to be permanent in their character.

GENERAL REGULATIONS Usages and Customs, Rules, Edicts and Resolutions are those Masonic rules of action adopted by the competent authority for local and/or temporary purposes, admitting of change at convenience, and not embraced in Ancient Landmarks or Constitutions. They are frequently termed By-Laws. When they so operate as to alter, modify or otherwise affect the Constitution, as defined in the preceding paragraph, they are also styled Constitutions.

THE MASONIC CONSTITUTION

Jurisprudence

Landmarks and in the Ancient Charges. Procedure is dealt with in the Book of Constitutions, and also, to some extent, in Grand Lodge decisions.

The Landmarks may be defined as There is enough Masonic law to warrant the term "Jurisprudence", which infers a system or body of law as opposed to an isolated rule. Others will associate the word "law" with our civil law with its prohibitions, penalties and sanctions. Masonry differs from the state in that the prohibitions are a matter of conscience, and the only sanctions are those of public opinion (The Craft) and the power of reprimand, suspension or expulsion from the membership. Be this as it may, Masonry has a system and body of law which goes back for many centuries. This system embraces both principles and procedure. The principles are to be found in two sources, in what we know as the ancient doctrines and customs that are essential to Masonry's Identity; remove a Landmark and Masonry would be something else. For this reason the Landmarks cannot be changed by any Mason, Lodge or

Grand Lodge. Being the fundamentals of Masonry, the Landmarks constitute its basic laws.

The Ancient Charges require adherence to the moral law, conformity to the laws of the country whose protection we invoke, thrift and honorable dealing in private life, courtesy, and the promotion of the social virtues; that is, working for the good of the community and of society at large. They also call for loyalty to Masonry as a whole, and to our Lodge and Grand Lodge in particular. The Master-elect of a Lodge must give his assent to a summary of the Ancient Charges before he can be installed. In addition, he is obliged to admit that it is not in the power of any man, or body of men, to make innovation in the body of Masonry. This is an all-important fact. Masonry has its roots far in the past, it has been proved in the fires of experience, and it survives today. There may be things which some think should be improved. Possibly they are right; but the result of change might be to create something other than Masonry. The structure of most Grand Lodges is based on the General Regulations adopted by the Grand Lodge of England shortly after it was created in the year 1717. The General Regulations contain these words: "Every Annual Grand Lodge has an inherent Power and Authority to make new Regulations, or to alter them, for the real benefit of this Ancient Fraternity; provided always that the old Landmarks be carefully preserved". The regulations of a Grand Lodge, therefore, are liable to amendment and change; in fact, they are amended fairly often.

Masonic Jurisprudence is also concerned with the bylaws of a Lodge. Although a Lodge may make its own bylaws, they must be consistent with the regulations of Grand Lodge and be approved by the Grand Master. Grand Lodge decisions and the edicts of Grand Masters also form part of the legal structure of Masonry. Thus, Masonic Jurisprudence includes written laws, decisions, edicts and unwritten laws, such as the Landmarks and other established practices of the Fraternity. The system is looser than the similar body of law for the government of a nation. Nevertheless, the Craft is well governed.

CHAPTER 3

Organization and Structure

Of

The Grand Lodge

"How it Works"

THE GRAND LODGE

What is the Grand Lodge?

Ironically, this question, to the well initiated may seem to be very simple, however, it is very legitimate. The profane may perceive it more genuinely then that of the defined craft, be this as it may, the question still remains " What is the Grand Lodge?" … To simply state, it is Governing body of all Masonic affiliates within its jurisdiction, having the overall lawful authority to act on any and all matters concerning its affiliates within that jurisdiction.

Powers and Authority of the Grand Lodge

SEC. 1-1 SUPREME MASONIC POWER.

The Grand Lodge is the *Supreme Masonic* power and authority in the state. It is the only legitimate authority under which Masonic Lodges can lawfully be congregated within its jurisdiction, and then only by virtue of a dispensation or a charter granted by it. It has all the attributes of sovereignty and government in matters Masonic, legislative executive, and judicial-limited only by provisions of its own Constitution and Regulations and by a careful adherence to the Ancient Landmarks.

SEC. 1-2 SOVEREIGNTY OF THE GRAND LODGE.

The sovereignty of the Grand Lodge touching upon all Masonic matters within, but not outside of, its territorial boundary is full and complete and any of its subordinate lodges has the right to receive the petition of any profane for the degrees or the application of any nonaffiliated Mason for affiliation who possess the physical, mental, moral, and residential qualifications that may be required by the Constitution, Regulations, and Laws of the Grand Lodge. No other grand lodge shall have or exercise any rights within the territorial jurisdiction of this Grand Lodge.

SEC. 1-3 OTHER GRAND LODGES.

This Grand Lodge concedes the same rights and powers to all other grand lodges within their respective jurisdictions.

SEC. 1-4 DEGREES.

By virtue of its sovereign and undelegated authority, this Grand Lodge is the creator of its subordinate lodges and is the repository of final and unimpeachable Masonic authority within all of its jurisdiction and is therefore, the absolute, exclusive, and indisputable owner and controller of the whole system of creed and symbolism of the degrees of Entered Apprentice Fellow Craft, and Master Mason. From this exclusive proprietorship all authority possessed by subordinate lodges or individuals in this state to assemble or to act in the capacity of Masons and in the name of Masonry is derived. Whatever superstructure is erected upon Symbolic Masonry in Tennessee stands upon the foundation, the groundwork, laid by the Grand Lodge.

SEC. 1-5 OTHER ORGANIZATIONS.

Masonic and/or any organization, association, or person/s within this state professing to have any authority, powers or privileges in Ancient Craft or Symbolic not derived from the Grand Lodge is declared to be clandestine, and all Masonic intercourse or with Masonic recognition of them or any of them, is prohibited.

SEC. 1-6 POWER OF THE GRAND LODGE.

The Grand Lodge has power to do whatsoever may be considered necessary to the well-being and perpetuity of Masonry within its jurisdiction, subject to the Landmarks and the provisions contained in its own Constitution and By-Laws, but particularly:

1. To grant dispensations and charters for holding lodges of Ancient, Free and Accepted Masons, with the right to confer therein the several degrees of Entered Apprentice, Fellow Craft, and Master Mason; and when deemed expedient and for good cause, it may arrest, suspend, annul, revoke, or amend such dispensations or charters or any preexisting dispensations or charters.

2. To exercise original and exclusive jurisdiction (1) over all subjects of Masonic legislation, interpretation, practice, and administration; (2) appellate, judicial, and administrative jurisdiction regarding decisions of the Grand Master, Masters, and Trial Commissions, and decisions and acts of lodges; (3) and when expedient, to exercise original judicial jurisdiction over its own officers and members, Masters, and Master Masons, Fellow Crafts, and Entered Apprentices within its jurisdiction. That is to say, the enactments and decisions of the Grand Lodge upon

all matters, things, and questions Masonic shall be the supreme Masonic law of the jurisdiction.

3. To define the territorial jurisdiction of each lodge, to change the same from time to time, to settle all controversies that may arise between lodges, and to make final decision and determination of all matters of controversy or grievances which may be brought before it by appeal or otherwise.

4. To make and adopt general and special laws and regulations for the government of its officers and members, and of the several subordinate lodges, their officers and members, and to alter, amend, or repeal the same.

5. To supervise the state and condition of its own finances and to adopt such measures in relation thereto as may be deemed necessary.

6. To reprimand, suspend, or expel any member from its own body for violation of its Constitution, Regulations or Laws, or for any unmasonic conduct; and it may reprimand, suspend, or expel any accused Mason upon appeal or restore one who has been suspended or expelled.

7. To consider and review the reports and doings of its officers, members of its committees, commissions, and boards, and of the several lodges under its jurisdiction and to take such action thereon as it may deem proper.

8. To establish, maintain, and enforce a uniform mode of work and lectures.

9. To declare by ordinary resolution which bodies in this jurisdiction acting in the name of Masonry are legitimate; and the moment an *independent rite or organization* begins to operate in the name of Masonry and is built meditatively or immediately upon the system of either or all of the three Symbolic degrees of Entered Apprentice, Fellow Craft, and Master Mason, the Grand Lodge has the right to pronounce judgment upon its legitimacy and to authorize or interdict Masonic intercourse therewith. No recognition will be presumed because the Grand Lodge has not expressly taken affirmative action in recognition or non-recognition thereof.

10. This Grand Lodge does not recognize as Masonic any body or organization merely because such body or organization is recognized by a body, rite, or organization which is recognized by the Grand Lodge.

11. Neither this Grand Lodge nor any of its subordinate lodges, nor any officer of either in his capacity as such officer, shall at any time act or serve as administrator, executor, guardian, trustee, or in any fiduciary capacity, *except* as expressly provided by the law of the Grand Lodge.

12. 12The powers expressed in this section, whether general or special, shall not limit or control any power or function so expressed, but each clause shall be construed in furtherance, and not in limitation, of powers anciently or otherwise exercised.

SEC. 1-7 JUDICIAL POWERS OF THE GRAND LODGE.

The judicial powers of the Grand Lodge may be exercised by it, or may be delegated, such powers are both original and appellate, embracing all matters of controversy and discipline in matters Masonic.

1. All trials of charges preferred and appeals taken in pursuance of the provisions of this Constitution shall be conducted in accordance with THE CODE of the Grand Lodge. [The Trial Code].

2. The rule that a penal statute, or one in derogation of the common law, is strictly construed does not apply to THE CODE or to the Trial Code, or to any of the provisions of either, but all such provisions must be construed according to the fair import of their terms to promote justice and effect their objects.

* NOTE: The sections number in this manual does not describe or indicate any particular order in which they may appear or be published in any jurisdictional constitution.

GRAND LODGE FOCUS

Support and Management Objectives

Summary Views:

- If Grand Lodge is to discharge its duty to the Craft, it must provide an administration that can meet all the needs of the Lodges under its jurisdiction.

- Its focus must be on the needs of members and Lodges.

- It must capture member support by pushing empowerment and accountability at all levels.

- It must aim for "the better good of the craft " throughout its administration.

- It must provide direction through a board equipped to concentrate on all the concerns of the Craft through an administrative structure that will attract and utilize input from all our members and their expertise.

Mechanism:

1. By a Grand Master elected on the basis of the best man to lead the Craft irrespective of the Division in which he resides and may be nominated by any District.

2. By A Board of General Purposes, reduced in size, but designed for the task with three elected members chosen irrespective of rank.

3. Master Masons as members of Grand Lodge contributing freely at Communication and at Divisional Conferences.

4. A voting regime of one vote per Lodge and no personal votes both at Communication and for the election of the Grand Master. Proxy votes able to be exercised.

5. A Communication and Grand Installation held every second year (a biennial Communication) with consequential financial saving to the Craft with separate Divisional Conferences held at least once a year.

6. Lodges electing their own District Grand Master on a two yearly basis.

7. Districts within each Division nominating their own Divisional Grand Master for appointment by the Grand Master for a three year term.

8. The return of power to the Lodges to influence policy and constitutional change.

9. A separation of administrative and ceremonial responsibilities in the servicing of Lodges using regional groupings within a semi-autonomous Divisional structure.

GRAND LODGE COMMITTEES

Often, there has been a misconception of the Grand Lodge. Many view it as a "high remote", Stupendous Tower, often times inaccessible, and 'The Power' which it imposes on its Lodges and members employed without conscience . Sound familiar? We'd like to dispel that view and what better way than through informative articles in Masonic News letters. This can be accomplished by the Grand setting up open lines of communication with its members by having such a resource. In this section, we'd like to take this opportunity and explain the organization of Grand Lodge and outline the way in which the Grand Lodge operates.

The Grand Lodge is not an entity on to itself, but is comprised of all the constituent lodges within its jurisdiction or state. Its function is to communicate and co-ordinate the activities of all the Lodges and affiliated bodies within its jurisdiction or state, preserve the time honored traditions of the Masonic fraternity, ensure adherence to the Constitution and Regulations, and acts as a 'Central Clearing House' between the constituent Lodges and the other Grand Lodges around the world. The Grand Lodge is a complex system of management that should and does operate like an industry of commerce, it comprise of various other committees, that may need to deal with a particular matter, work under the direction of a Governing Board, at times this board may be known as the "Board of Trustees" and, besides the regular members of the Board, may have non-Board members appointed to them because of their particular expertise in certain fields (e.g. Legal, Financial etc.) The Governing Board generally consists of all Past Grand Masters, the five elected Officers of Grand Lodge namely; The Grand Master, The Deputy Grand Master, Grand Senior Warden, Grand Junior Warden, Grand Treasurer, Grand Secretary/Registrar and one elected member from each of the districts in the jurisdiction. The Grand Secretary is usually the secretary of the Governing Board and of all sensitive committees under the Board (e.g. Finance, credentials etc.) and does not have any voting privileges on any of the actions of the Board or committees. The elected district members are also members of the Youth Programs Committee.

Committees

Administration and Finance – Has the responsible of examining and reporting on all of Grand Lodge's administrative and financial matters which are not the responsibility of another committee. All requests for appropriations of Grand Lodge funds must be made to the Committee. The duties include examining all of the records of the Grand Treasurer and Grand Secretary and submitting a report on the financial condition of Grand Lodge to each Annual Communication. Before the close of each Annual Communication, the Committee must present a detailed budget which estimates the receipts and expenses for the current year. In conjunction with the Grand Secretary and in accordance with the budget, the Committee is responsible for approving and ordering all printing, supplies, office equipment and regalia for Grand Lodge and its Officers.

<u>Appeals and Grievances</u> - Committee established to review all appeals, grievances and Complaints by members of the jurisdiction. To ensure that the Disposition of all matters handle or discharge conform to the Grand Lodge Constitution and standards of Masonic Jurisprudence.

<u>Auditing and Accounting</u> - May at times be referred to as the Finance committee, it serves as the Watch dog for the Grand Lodge in the maintenance of its financial Records, ensuring the proper bookkeeping of all receipts and Disbursements of all accounts in the name of the Grand Lodge.

<u>Budget and Rates</u> - May at times be referred to as the Committee on Ways and Means, established to review the feasibility aspect to Grand Lodge matters Concerning financial issues, to ensure that financial conditions are maintained as to the continuing sovereignty of the Grand Lodge and its capital status. It Reviews and analyze the current economic status to determine levels of increase and/or Decreases for rates paid to the Grand Lodge. Evaluating the time value of Money.

<u>Constitution</u> - Established to review the Grand Lodge Constitution, to ensure that all parts, sections and elements are current and checked for its accuracy. To resolve all matters of mis-Interpretation and/or confusion as to the written meaning of the Constitution or any Parts or sections. To ensure the inclusion of any and all amendments and changes as They properly accepted by the Grand Lodge.

<u>Credentials and Returns</u> - A committee established to certify and validate the voting privilege of subordinate Lodges that are in good financial standing with the Grand Lodge.

<u>Grand Master's Address</u> - The committee that is responsible for presenting to the Grand Lodge The Grand Master's Address for proper vote to be received in the Archives of the of the Grand Lodge. It is made up primarily of Past Grand Masters. Its prime duty is to consider and report on the Grand Master's annual address at Grand Lodge Communication each year. It critiques his message and reviews any recommendations he may make to ensure they are compatible with the Constitution and Regulations of the Grand Lodge. Another of its primary functions is to review and consider all motions for amending or altering the Constitution or Regulations and check for their regularity. This is why all proposed resolutions for the Annual Communication must be in the Grand Lodge office by the middle of February to be considered at the June Communication. It DOES NOT approve or disapprove any of these motions, but only ensures that they are in the proper form for formal consideration of the Brethren at the Annual Communication. It also confers with the Grand Master on all questions and decisions of Masonic law and usage presented to them for their approval and decision. Many of the decisions arrived at by this Committee ends up as 'Approved Rulings' in the Constitution.

<u>Fraternal Relations</u> - is "the Foreign Office" of the Grand Lodge. Its duty is to examine, with the assistance of the Grand Representatives, all the printed or written proceedings or documents from other Grand Lodges in correspondence with this Grand Lodge. It also is to report to each Annual Communication whatever it may deem of sufficient importance and interest to the Craft and make recommendations to Grand Lodge concerning the extension of recognition of other Grand Lodges by this Grand Lodge. This is usually done after a Grand Lodge makes application to this Grand Lodge for recognition. There are, at almost any given time, a number of positions open for Grand Representatives

to other jurisdictions and a phone call to the Grand Lodge office is all it takes to find out which ones are vacant.

Jurisprudence - Established to ensure that adherence to Masonic Law is applied in accordance With the Constitution and the historical practices and uses of the Ancient customs. To serve as counsel to the Grand Lodge in review of matters of Masonic charges Brought against members of the craft.

Necrology - A committee establish to gathering and assembling information of Brethren of the craft Who have past during the time since the last assembly of the Grand Lodge for the Purpose of paying tribute to them during the Grand Lodge Memorial Ceremony.

O. E. S. Visitation - The committee assigned by the Grand Master to coordinate with the Grand Chapter Order of Eastern Star for the visitation of the Grand Master and the Grand Lodge.

Public Relations - Perhaps one of the lesser known committees within the Grand Lodge but it has an important role in the operation of Grand Lodge. It is responsible for developing long range plans for public relations within our jurisdiction and for submitting them for consideration of the Board. Also, its duties include publicizing of special programs as directed by the Governing Board and providing direction and assistance to the Editor of the Grand Lodge News Letter and Special Bulletins, whom serves as a member of this committee.

Resolutions - Matters which shall be referred to the Committee on Masonic Jurisprudence and its duties relative to these and other things are as follows:

1. All proposals to amend the written law of the Grand Lodge shall be referred to the committee.

A.) It shall report its recommendations for action thereon to the Grand Lodge.

B.) It shall see that all such proposals, except those to amend the Constitution of the Grand Lodge, do not conflict with the provisions of that Constitution.

2. All decisions, opinions, and recommendations of the Grand Lodge on matters of Masonic law and usage shall be referred to this committee for review and forwarded to the committees on Constitution and Jurisprudence for their consideration . If in the opinion of the committee a point has been decided by the Grand Master which is not, but which should be made, a part of the written law and decision be not in proper form, therefore, the committee shall put it in proper form and submit it with its recommendations to the Grand Lodge.

3. The committee shall consider and report to the Grand Lodge on all other matters of legal significance referred to it by the Grand Lodge or by the Grand Master.

United Charities - This committee in some jurisdictions may not operate independent of itself, generally recommendations are received from other committees such as Public Relations and Fraternal Relations. The committee generally works with the Governing Board to evaluate the contributable efforts and recommend the limitations of contributions to specific campaigns and charities, which those recommendation are forwarded to the committee on Budget and Rates for consideration and review of the feasibility of the recommendation.

<u>Warrants and Dispensations</u> - The following matters shall be referred to this committee:

1. All petitions to change the name or location of a subordinate lodge.
2. All petitions for duplicate charters.
3. All petitions for charters by lodges under dispensation.
4. All petitions to change territorial jurisdiction of lodges.

The duties of the Committee on Charters and Dispensations shall be as follows:

1. To review and report to the Grand Lodge with their recommendations on all matters referred to it.

2. To examine the records of proceedings and work done by each lodge under dispensation and to make a report to the Grand Lodge on the correctness and regularity thereof, together with recommendations, and such information as it deems pertinent which may include the opinion of the committee as to the proficiency in the ritualistic work, knowledge of the law, and disposition to obey it, of the lodge under dispensation. If a charter is recommended in its report, it shall state the name, number and location, as well as the names, in full, of the first three principal officers of the new lodge.

OFFICERS of the GRAND LODGE

*The MOST WORSHIPFUL GRAND MASTER

*RIGHT WORSHIPFUL DEPUTY GRAND MASTER

*Right Worshipful Grand Senior Warden

*Right Worshipful Grand Junior Warden

Right Worshipful Grand Senior Deacon

Right Worshipful Grand Junior Deacon

*Right Worshipful Grand Treasurer

*Right Worshipful Grand Secretary

Right Worshipful Grand Senior Stewart

Right Worshipful Grand Junior Stewart

Right Worshipful Grand Chaplain

Right Worshipful Grand Marshall

Right Worshipful Grand Lecturer

Right Worshipful Grand Master of Ceremonies

*Right Worshipful Grand Tiler

Right Worshipful District Deputy Grand Masters (Districts)

*Denotes elected officers for most Prince Hall Jurisdictions

ORGANIZATION of the GRAND LODGE

STRUCTURE

The Grand Lodge

| Grand OES Chapter | Subordinate Lodge | Grand Chapter Royal Arch |

Grand OES Chapter

Grand Commandery Knights Templar

Grand OES Chapter

A.A.S.R.

Grand OES Chapter

Shrine A.E.A.O.N.M.S.

Masonic Youth Order

CHAPTER 4

The Landmarks
Of
Freemasonry

"What's Written and Unwritten"

THE LANDMARKS OF FREEMASONRY

"The Landmarks of Freemasonry are unwritten laws that form the basis of every Grand and subordinate Lodge constitution. The Landmarks are the foundation on which Freemasonry stands. The majority of Grand Lodges adopt all or a portion of the Landmarks listed below. An extensive discussion of these Masonic principals can be found in "Jurisprudence of Freemasonry."

Albert G. Mackey.

LANDMARK FIRST

The modes of RECOGNITION are, of all the Landmarks, the most legitimate and unquestioned. They admit of no variation; and if ever they have suffered alteration or addition, the evil of such a violation of the ancient law has always made itself subsequently manifest. An admission of this is to be found in the proceedings of the Masonic Congress at Paris, where a proposition was presented to render these modes of recognition once more universal - a proposition which never would have been necessary, if the integrity of this important Landmark had been rigorously preserved.

LANDMARK SECOND

THE DIVISION OF SYMBOLIC MASONRY INTO THREE DEGREES is a Landmark that has been better preserved than almost any other, although even here the mischievous spirit of innovation has left its traces, and by the disruption of its concluding portion from the Third Degree, a want of uniformity has been created in respect to the final teaching of the Master's order, and the Royal Arch of England, Scotland, Ireland, and America, and the "high degrees" of France and Germany, are all made to differ in the mode in which they lead the neophyte to the great consummation of all symbolic masonry. In 1813, the Grand Lodge of England vindicated the ancient Landmark, by solemnly enacting that ancient craft Masonry consisted of the three degrees: Entered Apprentice, Fellow Craft, and Master Mason, including the Holy Royal Arch; but the disruption has never been healed, and the Landmark, although acknowledged in its integrity by all, still continues to be violated.

LANDMARK THIRD

The Legend of the THIRD DEGREE is an important Landmark, the integrity of which has been well preserved. There is no rite of Masonry, practiced in any country or language, in which the essential elements of this legend are not taught. The lectures may vary, and indeed are constantly changing, but the legend has ever remained substantially the same; and it is necessary that it should be so, for the legend of the Temple Builder constitutes the very essence and identity of Masonry; any rite which should exclude it, or materially alter it, would at once, by that exclusion or alteration, cease to be a Masonic rite.

LANDMARK FOURTH

THE GOVERNMENT OF THE FRATERNITY BY A PRESIDING OFFICER called a Grand Master, who is elected from the body of the craft, is a Fourth Landmark of the Order. Many persons ignorantly suppose that the election of the Grand Master is held in consequence of a law or regulation of the Grand Lodge. Such, however, is not the case. The office is indebted for its existence to a Landmark of the Order. Grand Masters are to be found in the records of the institution long before Grand Lodges were established; and if the present system of legislative government by Grand Lodges were to be abolished, a Grand Master would be necessary. In fact, although there has been a period within the records of history, and indeed of very recent date, when a Grand Lodge was unknown, there never has been a time when the craft did not have their Grand Master.

LANDMARK FIFTH

The prerogative of the Grand Master to preside over every assembly of the craft, where so ever and when so ever held, is a fifth Landmark. It is in consequence of this law, derived from ancient usage, and not from any special enactment, that the Grand Master assumes the chair, or as it is called in England, "the throne," at every communication of the Grand Lodge; and that he is also entitled to preside at the communication of every Subordinate Lodge, where he may happen to be present.

LANDMARK SIXTH

The Prerogative of the Grand Master to grant Dispensations for conferring degrees at irregular times, is another and a very important Landmark. The statutory law of Masonry requires a month, or other determinate period, to elapse between the presentation of a petition and the election of a candidate. But the Grand Master has the power to set aside or dispense with this probation, and allow a candidate to be initiated at once. This prerogative he possessed in common with all Masters, before the enactment of the law requiring a probation, and as no statute can impair his prerogative, he still retains the power, although the Masters of Lodges no longer possess it.

LANDMARK SEVENTH

The prerogative of the Grand Master to give dispensations for opening and holding Lodges is another Landmark. He may grant, in virtue of this, to a sufficient number of Masons, the privilege of meeting together and conferring degrees. The Lodges thus established are called "Lodges under Dispensation." They are strictly creatures of the Grand Master, created by his authority, existing only during his will and pleasure, and liable at any moment to be dissolved at his command. They may be continued for a day, a month, or six months; but whatever be the period of their existence, they are indebted for that existence solely to the grace of the Grand Master.

LANDMARK EIGHTH

The prerogative of the Grand Master to make masons at sight, is a Landmark which is closely connected with the preceding one. There has been much misapprehension in relation to this Landmark, which misapprehension has sometimes led to a denial of its existence in jurisdictions where the Grand Master was perhaps at the very time substantially exercising the prerogative, without the slightest remark or opposition. It is not to be supposed that the Grand Master can retire with a profane into a private room, and there, without assistance, confer the degrees of Freemasonry upon him. No such prerogative exists, and yet many believe that this is the so much talked of right of "making Masons at sight". The real mode and the only mode of exercising the prerogative is this: The Grand Master summons to his assistance not less than six other masons, convenes a Lodge, and without any previous probation, but on sight of the candidate, confers the degrees upon him. after which he dissolves the Lodge. and dismisses the brethren. Lodges thus convened for special purposes are called occasional lodges," This is the only way in which any Grand Master within the records of the institution has ever been known to "make a Mason at sight". The prerogative is dependent upon that of granting dispensations to open and hold Lodges. If the Grand Master has the power of granting to any other Mason the privilege of presiding over Lodges working by his dispensation, he may assume this privilege of presiding to himself; and as no one can deny his right to revoke his dispensation granted to a number of brethren at a distance, and to dissolve the Lodge at his pleasure, it will scarcely be contended that he may not revoke his dispensation for a Lodge over which he himself has been presiding, within a day, and dissolve the Lodge as soon as the business for which he had assembled it is accomplished. The making of Masons at sight is only the conferring of the degrees by the Grand Master, at once, in an occasional Lodge, constituted by his dispensing power for the purpose, and over which he presides in person.

LANDMARK NINTH

The necessity of masons to congregate in lodges is another Landmark. It is not to be understood by this that any ancient Landmark has directed that permanent organization of subordinate Lodges which constitutes one of the features of the Masonic system as it now prevails, but the landmarks of the Order always prescribed that Masons should from time to time congregate together, for the purpose of either operative or speculative labor, and that these congregations should be called Lodges. Formerly these were extemporary meetings called together for special purposes, and then dissolved, the brethren departing to meet again at other times and other places, according to the necessity of circumstances. But warrants of constitution, by-laws, permanent officers and annual arrears, are modern innovations wholly outside of the Landmarks, and dependent entirely on the special enactments of a comparatively recent period.

LANDMARK TENTH

The government of the craft, when so congregated in a Lodge by a Master and two Wardens, is also a Landmark. To show the influence of this ancient law, it may be observed by the way, that a congregation of Masons meeting together under any other government, as that for instance of a president and vice-president, or a chairman and sub-chairman, would not be recognized as a Lodge, The presence of a Master and two Wardens is as essential to the valid organization of a Lodge as a warrant of constitution is at the present day. The names, of course, vary in different languages, the Master, for instance, being called "Venerable" in French Masonry, and the Wardens "Surveillants," but the officers, their number, prerogatives and duties, are everywhere identical.

LANDMARK ELEVENTH

The necessity that every lodge, when congregated, should be duly tiled, is an important Landmark of the institution, which is never neglected. The necessity of this law arises from the esoteric character of Masonry. As a secret institution, its portals must of course be guarded from the intrusion of the profane, and such a law must therefore always have been in force from the very beginning of the Order. It is therefore properly classed among the most ancient Landmarks. The office of Tiler is wholly independent of any special enactment of Grand or Subordinate Lodges, although these may and do prescribe for him additional duties, which vary in different jurisdictions. But the duty of guarding the door, and keeping off cowans and eavesdroppers, is an ancient one, which constitutes a Landmark for the government.

LANDMARK TWELFTH

The right of every mason to be represented in all general meetings of the craft and to instruct his representatives, is a twelfth Landmark. Formerly, these general meetings, which were usually held once a year, were called "General Assemblies," and all the fraternity, even to the youngest Entered Apprentice, were permitted to be present. Now they are called "Grand Lodges," and only the Masters and Wardens of the Subordinate Lodges are summoned. But this is simply as the representatives of their members. Originally, each Mason represented himself; now he is represented by his officers. was a concession granted by the fraternity about 1717, and of course does not affect the integrity of the Landmark, for the principle of representation is still preserved. The concession was only made for purposes of convenience.

LANDMARK THIRTEEN

The Right of every mason to appeal from the decision of his brethren in Lodge convened, to the Grand Lodge or General Assembly of Masons, is a Landmark highly essential to the preservation of justice, and the prevention of oppression. A few modern Grand Lodges, in adopting a regulation that the decision of Subordinate Lodges, in cases of expulsion, cannot be wholly set aside upon an appeal, have violated this unquestioned Landmark, as well as the principles of just government

LANDMARK FOURTEENTH

THE RIGHT OF EVERY MASON TO VISIT and sit in every regular Lodge is an unquestionable Landmark of the Order." This is called "the right of visitation." This right of visitation has always been recognized as an inherent right, which inures to every Mason as he travels through the world. And this is because Lodges are justly considered as only divisions for convenience of the universal Masonic family. This right may, of course be impaired or forfeited on special occasions by various circumstances; but when admission is refused to a Mason in good standing, who knocks at the door of a Lodge as a visitor, it is to be expected that some good and sufficient reason shall be furnished for this violation, of what is in general a Masonic right, founded on the Landmarks of the Order.

LANDMARK FIFTEENTH

It is a Landmark of the Order, that no visitor, unknown to the brethren present, or to some one of them as a Mason, can enter a Lodge without first passing an examination according to ancient usage. Of course, if the visitor is known to any brother present to be a Mason in good standing, and if that brother will vouch for his qualifications, the examination may be dispensed with, as the Landmark refers only to the cases of strangers, who are not to be recognized unless after strict trial, due examination, or lawful information.

LANDMARK SIXTEENTH

No Lodge can interfere in the business of another Lodge, nor give degrees to brethren who are members of other Lodges, This is undoubtedly an ancient Landmark, founded on the great principles of courtesy and fraternal kindness, which are at the very foundation of our institution. It has been repeatedly recognized by subsequent statutory enactments of all Grand Lodges.

LANDMARK SEVENTEENTH

It is a Landmark that every freemason is Amenable to the Laws and Regulations of the Masonic jurisdiction in which he resides, and this although he may not be a member of any Lodge. Non-affiliation, which is, in fact in itself a Masonic offence, does not exempt a Mason from Masonic Jurisdiction.

LANDMARK EIGHTEENTH

Certain qualifications of candidates for initiation are derived from a Landmarks of the Order. These qualifications are that he shall be a man, shall be unmutilated, free born, and of mature age. That is to say, a woman, a cripple, or a slave, or one born in slavery, is disqualified for initiation into the rites of Masonry. Statutes, it is true, have from time to time been enacted, enforcing or explaining these principles; but the qualifications really arise from the very nature of the Masonic institution, and from its symbolic teachings, and have always existed as landmarks.

LANDMARK NINETEENTH

A belief in the existence of God as the GRAND ARCHITECT of the universe, is one of the most important Landmarks of the Order. It has been always deemed essential that a denial of the existence of a Supreme and Superintending Power, is an absolute disqualification for initiation. The annals of the Order never yet have furnished or could furnish an instance in which an avowed atheist was ever made a Mason. The very Initiatory ceremonies of the first degree forbid and prevent the possibility of so monstrous an occurrence.

LANDMARK TWENTIETH

Subsidiary to this belief in God, as a Landmark of the Order, is the belief in a resurrection to a future life. This Landmark is not so positively impressed on the candidate by exact words as the preceding; but die doctrine is taught by very plain implication, and runs through the whole symbolism of the Order. To believe in Masonry, and not to believe in a resurrection, would be an absurd anomaly, which could only be excused by the reflection, that he who thus confounded his belief and his skepticism, was so ignorant of the meaning of both theories as to have no rational foundation for his knowledge of either.

LANDMARK TWENTY-FIRST

It is a Landmark, that a "Book of the Law" shall constitute an indispensable part of the furniture of every Lodge. I say advisedly, a Book of the Law, because it is not absolutely required that everywhere the Old and New Testaments shall be used. The "Book of the Law" is that volume which, by the religion of the country, is believed to contain the revealed will of the Grand Architect Of The Universe. Hence, in all Lodges in Christian countries, the Book of the Law is composed of the Old and New Testaments; in a country where Judaism was the prevailing faith, the Old Testament alone would be sufficient; and in Mohammedan countries, and among Mohammedan Masons the Koran might be substituted. Masonry does not attempt to interfere with the peculiar religious faith of its disciples, except so far as relates to the belief in the existence of God, and what necessarily results from that belief." The Book of the Law is to the speculative Mason his spiritual Trestle-board; without this he cannot labor; whatever he believes to be the revealed will of the Grand Architect constitutes for him this spiritual Trestle- board, and must ever be before him in his hours of speculative labor, to be the rule and guide of his conduct The Landmark, therefore, requires that a Book of the Law, a religious code of some kind, purporting to be an exemplar of the revealed will of God, shall form in essential part of the furniture of every Lodge.

LANDMARK TWENTY-SECOND

THE EQUALITY OF ALL MASONS is another Landmark of the Order. This equality has no reference to any subversion of those gradations of rank which have been instituted by the usages of society. The monarch, the nobleman or the gentleman is entitled to all the influence, and receives all the respect which rightly belong to his exalted position. But the doctrine of Masonic equality implies that, as children of one great Father, we meet in the Lodge upon the level-that on that level we are all traveling to one predestined goal, that in the Lodge genuine merit shall receive more respect than boundless wealth, and that virtue and knowledge alone should be the basis of all Masonic honors, and be rewarded with preferment When the labors of the Lodge are over, and the brethren have retired from their peaceful retreat, to mingle once more with the world, each will then again resume that social position, and exercise the privileges of that rank, to which the customs of society entitle him.

LANDMARK TWENTY-THIRD

The secrecy of the institution is another and a most important Landmark. There is some difficulty in precisely defining what is meant by a "secret society," If the term refers, as perhaps in strictly logical language it should, to those associations whose designs are concealed from the public eye, and whose members are unknowing which produce their results in darkness, and whose operations are carefully hidden from the public gaze - a definition which will be appropriate to many political clubs and revolutionary combinations in despotic countries, where reform, if it is at all to be effected, must be effected by stealth - then clearly Freemasonry is not a secret society. Its design is not only publicly proclaimed. But is vaunted by its disciples as something to be venerated; its disciples are known, for its membership is considered an honor to be coveted; it works for a result of which it boasts, the civilization, and reformation of his manners. But if by a Secret society is meant, and this is the most popular understanding of the term, a society in which there is a certain amount of knowledge, whether it be of methods of recognition, or of legendary and traditional learning, which is imported to those only who have passed through an established form of initiation, the form itself being also concealed or esoteric, then in this sense is Freemasonry undoubtedly a secret society. Now this form of secrecy is a form inherent in it, existing with It from its very foundation, and secured to it by its ancient Landmarks. If divested of its secret character, it would lose its identity, and would cease to be Freemasonry. whatever objections may, therefore, be made to the institution, on account of its secrecy, and however much some unskillful brethren have been willing in times of trial, for the sake of expediency, to divest it of its secret character, it will be ever impossible to do so, even were die Landmark not standing before us as an insurmountable obstacle; because such change of its character would be social suicide, and the death of the

Order would follow its legalized exposure. Freemasonry, as a secret association, has lived unchanged for centuries an open society it would not last for as many years.

LANDMARK TWENTY-FOURTH

The foundation of a Speculative Science upon an Operative Art, and these symbolic uses and explanations of the terms of that art, for purposes of religious or moral teaching, constitute another Landmark of the Order. The Temple of Solomon was the cradle of the institution," and, therefore, the reference to the operative Masonry, which constructed that magnificent edifice, to the materials and implements which were employed in its construction, and to the artists who were engaged in the building, are all component and essential parts of the body of Freemasonry, which could not be subtracted from it without an entire destruction of the whole identity of the Order. Hence, all the comparatively modern rites of Masonry, however they may differ in other respects, religiously preserve this temple history and these operative elements, as the substratum of all their modifications of the Masonic system.

LANDMARK TWENTY-FIFTH

The last and crowning Landmark of all is, that these Landmarks can never be changed. Nothing can be subtracted from them-nothing can be added to them-not the slightest modification can be made in them. As they were received from our predecessors, we are bound by the most solemn obligations of duty to transmit them to our successors. Not one jot or one title of these unwritten laws can be repealed; for in respect to them, we are not only willing but compelled to adopt the language of the sturdy old barons of England - "Nolumus legen mutari."

CHAPTER 5

Workings of the
Bluehouse Lodge

"The Who and What it is"

THE "BLUEHOUSE" LODGE

What is a LODGE ?

To immediately dispose of the notion that a Lodge is a Building where Masons meets or assemble for the workings of a Lodge, is false. Too often emphasis is and has been placed on the physical structure that's supports the organization rather than what the purpose of the organization really is. This is due to several reasons, for our purpose, we will only explore one. One of simply misunderstanding... The physical address of a Lodge serves solely the purpose of control, only to the extinct of having a known location that all members of the Lodge is aware of, this cuts down on where each time and all members of the Lodge know when and where the assembly is to take place. "*Whereby, the required number are present and those authorized to legitimize the assembly are present, constitute a Lodge.*"

The members of this organization present at its assemblies is what truly makes-up the Lodge. This is supported by defined "Ancient" customs as we have learned in previous exploits of where *our ancient brethren have met.* The assemblies that a Lodge organizes are with valued and constructive purpose. All of its members are volunteers in their service, therefore, assembled Lodges should have or at its interim should move to create an objective focus for its existence.

It is extremely important that all members understand the objectives of his Lodge, and for those members to convey and stress to those who may solicit membership, without detailed actions of implementation, that his membership is for the service of the Lodge and not self-serving.

It is the responsibility of the Officers elected and appointed to ensure that its members and the Lodge itself have a direct and clear focus for the improvement of its community by raising the spirit of unity and brotherhood through objective reasoning and education.

Structure of The Lodge
The Wor. Master

All activities are under his control
And when present at any assembly or
Committee Meeting serves as the "Chair"
Especially the committees on Budget and Finance

Sr. Warden	Jr. Warden
Serves as Chair for the following Committees;	Serves as Chair for the following Committees;
By-Laws	Fraternal Assistance
Audit	Jurisprudence
Investigation (Candidate)	Scholarship/Charity
Fraternal Relations	Events/Activities

Tiler
Serves as Chair of the Building Committee

In the best interest of the Lodge, all other member appointments to these committees should be by open solicitation to the entire Lodge, However, the Master, at his discretion, may make special appointment of those members of particular expertise in some cases where their experience would better serve the Lodge.

These committees are but a few that a Lodge may employ, they are based on the overall objectives of the lodge as a whole which best supports the views of all members and the focus of the Lodge.

The description of these committees are further discussed later in this chapter. What's more important to remember here is that it is the working members what makes up the Lodge and how effective they discharge the duties in their charge will ultimately determine how successful the Lodge will be.

DUTIES OF THE BLUE LODGE OFFICERS

Every well governed society and or organization consist of principle figures whom for the most part, act as organizers, controllers, counselors and overseers, be they whom they may. Freemasonry accepts this practice without prejudice and expands on its establishment as a genuine system of Democracy within its walls. Leaders of Masonic bodies are place in those positions based on their merit and not their seniority. This is accomplished by a majority vote of the members present or through their proxy, in their opinion, exercising their right as being financial in their standing, and through their character, the trust that they exert toward those men whom they nominate.

The Blue Lodge structure of principle Officers consist of both Elective and Appointed officers. These Trusted Officers have a duty and a responsibility to all members of the Lodge equally. It is the duty and responsibility of all members to support the efforts of the Officers Elected and or Appointed. Every member of the Lodge should have as his desire to occupy a leadership role within his Lodge and ultimately the seat in the EAST.

The WORSHIPFUL MASTER

The Worshipful Master is that Elected Officer who holds the highest office within the Lodge, The position of the highest Honor which can be bestowed upon a Master Mason. No Mason should begin climbing the flight of stairs to the Master's Chair in the East without first pledging to Himself that he will dedicate and devote all his energy and zeal to fulfilling his duties to the best of his ability. The trust placed upon him by the Brethren should never be violated. The Master of a Lodge must be a moral and Goodman; He is an exemplar to his flock. In his daily walk and conversation, he fail to practice out of the Lodge what he teaches in it, his labor is vain. The High seat is but a shadowy throne. The Lodge is a body without a head. How absurd to suppose that an immoral man can teach morality. The Master of the Lodge is Law abiding; In all mobs of public lawlessness of every form, in all violations of statute and common law by which the current history of our country is disgraced, he should be found at the lead in the preservation of public order. The service of the Master is for all and to all thereof, The Master of the Lodge.....

- Must be no conspirator or secret enemy of the Government
- Must be of good report before the community
- Must be temperate and meek
- Must be cautious, courteous, and faithful, and must practice self-government.
- Must possess an ardent love for genuine Masonry.
- Must respect Masonic superiors.
- Must be a zealous Mason.
- Must be versed in the Landmarks of Masonry.
- Must be a lover of the old-time things.

- Must be zealous of its honor.
- Must communicate statedly with the Grand Lodge.
- Must recognize no clandestine rivals.
- Must maintain the regularity of the Masonic system as essential to the very life and usefulness of Masonry itself.

PREROGATIVES OF THE WORSHIPFUL MASTER

The prerogatives of the Worshipful Master are so numerous, so varied, and so interwoven with one another, it is difficult to lay them out as so many threads from a tangled skein, and discuss them separately. For convenience we divide them into fourteen sections:

(Macoy's Worshipful Master Assistance)

I.   It is the prerogative of the W.M. to congregate (call together) his Lodge at his discretion.

II.   It is the prerogative of the W.M. to preside at all communications of his Lodge, whether regular or called, when present.

III.   It is the prerogative of the W.M. to fill all vacancies that may occur in the roster of his Lodge.

IV.   It is the prerogative of the W.M. to regulate the admission of visitors.

V.   It is the prerogative of the W.M. to control and terminate discussions.

VI.   It is the prerogative of the W.M. to determine all questions of order and the order of business without appeal, save to the Grand Master or Grand Lodge.

VII.   It is the prerogative of the W.M. to appoint all committees.

VIII.   It is the prerogative of the W.M. to be custodian of the Charter (Warrant)

IX.   It is the prerogative of the W.M. to order the issuance of notifications requiring the attendance of members.

X.   It is the prerogatives of the W.M. to give the casting vote in case of a tie, in addition to his own.

XI.   It is the prerogative of the W.M. to sign all drafts upon the treasure, for the payment of Lodge disbursements, by consent of the Lodge.

XII.   It is the prerogative of the W.M. to represent the Lodge in Grand Lodge, in conjunction with the two Wardens.

XIII.   It is the prerogative of the W.M. to appoint the Senior Deacon and such other Officers as may be prescribed in the By-Laws of the Lodge.

XIV.   It is the prerogative of the W.M. to install his successor.

Duties of the Worshipful Master

1. It is the duty of the W.M. to attend the regularly the communications of his lodge.

2. It is the duty of the W.M. to open his Lodge at the time specified in the By-Laws, and close it at a suitable hour.

3. It is the duty of the W.M. to preserve order in the Lodge.

4. It is the duty of the W.M. to regulate the admissions of visitors.

5. It is the duty of the W.M. to preserve the Charter of the Lodge inviolate, and transmit it to his successor.

6. It is the duty of the W.M. to perform the ritualistic work of the Lodge, and instruct the Brethren therein.

7. It is the duty of the W.M. to cause an investigation into all unmasonic conduct committed by persons affiliated with his Lodge; also of non-affiliated and members of other Lodges resident within his jurisdiction.

8. It is the duty of the W.M. to visit the sick and preside at the funeral rites of deceased Masons (when requested by his survivors or called).

9. It is the duty of the W.M. to use his utmost endeavors to preserve peace and harmony in his Lodge; and by his own deportment both within and without the Lodge, to be a good example to his Brethren.

The Wardens

The Wardens, in theory, are "two officers in a state of preparation for the Mastership." As it cannot be known when the W.M. will be absent, the language directed to the Senior Warden in the Installation Service is particularly applicable. "Your regular attendance at stated meeting is essentially necessary. In the absence of the Master he is to govern the Lodge; in his presence he is to assist him in the government of it." The Senior Warden is elected annually, and chosen not for his seniority, but for his merit. His specific powers and duties are thus:

1. To succeed to exercise all the powers of the W.M. in the event of the Master's absence.

2. To represent the Lodge in conjunction with the W.M. and J.W. at all the Grand L Communications of the Grand Lodge, when such rule prevails.

3. To act on the standing committee of Charity.

4. To appoint the Junior Deacon (this rule is not universal).

5. To take charge of the craft during the hours of labor.

The Junior Warden

The Junior Warden, like his immediate superior , is annually elected, not by his seniority, but by his merit. He must be a Master Mason, and a member of the Lodge. His specific powers and duties are thus:

1. To succeed to and exercise all the powers of the W.M. in the absence of the two officers above him.

2. To represent the Lodge in conjunction with the W.M. and S.W., at all the Grand Communications of the Grand Lodge, where this rule prevails.

3. To act on standing Committees of Charity.

4. To take charge of the craft during the hours of refreshments.

The Treasurer

This office, not the secretary, is the Lodge banker and should adhere to good business practice and habits. Receipts, records, monthly reports of expenditures and income, and proper investment of Lodge funds are his responsibility and duty to the Lodge. It is his duty to :

1. Receive all moneys from the Secretary and issue a receipt for the same.

2. Keep a just and regular account of the same.

3. Pay out money only by order of the Worshipful Master and consent of the Lodge.

4. Give an annual account to the Lodge.

5. Deliver all Lodge funds, books, vouchers, and written records and documents to his successor.

The Secretary

The duties of the secretary and the importance of his office cannot be emphasized too strongly. This is an office of confidence and respect. The secretary is the ambassador of good will and an administrator of Lodge affairs. His records are a part of the story of the Lodge. Prompt attendance to all business, neat and complete minutes and records are a must for this office. A secretary should never be late at the meetings, but be there in time to have everything in readiness, so the business may be conducted at the pleasure of the Master. The secretary should familiarize himself with his duties in the Book of Constitutions and By-laws and Secretaries Handbook. It is his duty to:

1. Observe the will and pleasure of the Worshipful Master.

2. Record all proceedings of the Lodge proper to be written.

3. Receive all moneys paid into the Lodge

4. Pay them over to the Treasurer taking his receipt thereof.

5. File all Documents of the Lodge.

6. Collect all dues of the Lodge and issue receipts.

7. Make monthly and annual reports on time to the Lodge and to the Grand Lodge.

8. Keep an up-to-date register of all members.

9. Keep in trust the Seal of the Lodge.

10. Perform all duties se forth in the Secretaries handbook.

11. Deliver to his successor all books, papers, records, vouchers, etc.

The Chaplain

The textbook of the Chaplain is that Great Light in Freemasonry which forever sheds its rays upon every lawful assemblage of Masons. He has the obvious duties to:

1. Open and close all meetings with prayer being careful to keep all supplications universal and common to all religions.

2. Attend all Masonic funeral services and give the prayers of that service.

3. Learn and deliver the scripture readings for the various degrees.

The Senior Deacon

The Senior Deacon is the messenger of the Worshipful Master. His most important duty is to welcome visiting Brethren and introduce them to the Lodge members so that they will feel at home. Both ritual and floor work are a part of the required operation of this station. He should be prepared to:

1. Introduce and accommodate the visitors of the Lodge.

2. Receive and conduct candidates in all degrees.

3. Prepare the ballot box at the order of the Worshipful Master.

4. Be able to give or assist with the Senior Deacon's (middle chamber) lecture.

5. Proceed with the study of the Book of Constitutions and By-laws and the By-laws of the Lodge.

6. Attend and participate in the Lodge schools of instruction.

7. Carry out the duties assigned by the Worshipful Master.

8. Commit to memory the Worshipful Master part of the Entered Apprentice Degree.

The Junior Deacon

It shall be the duty of the Junior Deacon to be the messenger of the Senior Warden. His duty is the custody of the door opening from the Tyler's room. He permits no one to enter or retire without consent from the Master or Senior Warden. He should be prepared to:

1. Understudy of the Senior Deacon that he may relieve him whenever necessary and prepare himself for advancement to the duties of the Senior Deacon including the committal and delivery of the Senior Deacon's degree work.

2. Assist in the preparation of the candidate for the degrees.

3. Reach a high degree of proficiency with the rod and floor work.

4. Assist in introducing visiting Brethren and see that they feel at home.

5. Proceed with a study of the Book of Constitutions and By-laws.

6. Attend all called meetings of the Lodge except when he has been officially excused.

7. Carry out Lodge assignments given by the Worshipful Master.

The Senior Steward

A good Lodge will be recognized when giving value to the work of the Stewards. It shall be the duty of the Senior Steward to assist the Deacons and other officers in the discharge of their duties, and to see that the tables are properly furnished at refreshment, and that every Brother is suitably provided for. It is his duty to:

1. Prepare and present candidates and to assist the Deacons and other officers in performing their duties.
2. Aid in making visitors feel welcome through introductions and providing a good seat n the Lodge Room.
3. Become proficient in rod and floor work.
4. Attend to other such duties as may be directed by the Worshipful Master.
5. Deliver memory lectures of all three degrees.

The Junior Steward

It shall be the duty of the Junior Steward to cheerfully accept the responsibility of aiding and assisting the Senior Steward. He should be prepared to:

1. Become proficient in rod and floor work.
2. Assist the Junior Warden when the Lodge is at refreshment.
3. Extend to visiting Brethren such attentions as circumstances may suggest.
4. Learn and deliver memory lectures of all three degrees.
5. Be punctual in attendance at all Lodge meetings , and assist the Senior Steward to prepare and present the candidate.

The Tiler

The appointment of the Tiler to the Lodge is of extreme importance especially if the progression to the Office of Master is practiced. Just as the Tyler's Sword is used as a symbol to guard against the approach of cowans and eavesdroppers, so should it admonish us to set a guard over our thoughts, words and actions, thereby preventing the approach of every unworthy thought, word, or deed and preserving consciences void of offense toward God and man. He should be prepared to:

1. Be prompt and early at all Lodge meetings and see that all Lodge paraphernalia is in place for all Stated, Called, and Special meeting.

2. See that all paraphernalia is kept clean and in good repair.

3. Assist the Senior Deacon and the Lodge Welcoming Committee to accommodate all visiting Brethren and act as host of the Lodge.

4. Inform the Master of a visiting Brother to be examined for admission.

5. See that all Brethren in the Lodge Room are properly clothed.

6. Register all regular and visiting Brethren and see that they are properly vouched for or examined.

7. See that all paraphernalia is put away at the close of Lodge.

Special Committees

The working Committees in Blue Lodges are the same as those Standing Committees at the Grand Lodge level, or at least some of them, Blue Lodges do not require that extensive number of Committees for its administration as that of the Grand Lodge. However, the same efforts are taken in the development and operation no matter what the level. These Committees are assigned and work for the better good of the Lodge as with the committees of the Grand Lodge. Constructive planning of the works of these Committees are vital to the productivity of the Lodge. Masters should take into account the abilities of the members of his Lodge when selecting, assigning and making appointments, to make better use out of the members that he has at his disposal. Below is a list of just a few committees that can be found in a Bluehouse Lodge; expanded definitions for some of these committees can be found in the section covering Committees of the Grand Lodge.

1. Budget and Finance Committee – Assigned to assist in the development of the budget and maintenance of the Lodge financial Records, ensuring the proper bookkeeping of all receipts and Disbursements are accurate and the appropriation of said funds are not abused.

2. By-Laws Committee - Appointed to review By-laws of the Lodge and ensure compliance to the constitution of the Grand Lodge.

3. Scholarship/Charity Committee - That committee appointed to review all request to the Lodge from those organization requesting assistance evaluate those eligible candidates for scholarship award and make final recommendation to the Lodge for its selection.

4. Building Committee – That committee appointed to review all items regarding usages, maintenance and municipal relations of the Lodge Hall and submit all request and necessary information and notices the Lodge for actions to be taken beyond the scope of authority granted the committee.

5. Audit Committee – Closely related to the finance committee, however, this committee's sole purpose is to review all books , financial and administrative records. To ensure that the books are all accounted for and in proper order for final audit by the Grand Lodge at the end of the Masonic year.

6. Investigation Committee – That committee appointed to conduct the personal interview of all eligible candidates requesting membership and reporting back to the Lodge its recommendation favorable or unfavorable of the moral character of each individual candidate.

7. Events/Activities Committee – A committee or committees appointed to review the feasibility of proposed and planned events and/ or activities and make final recommendation to the Lodge of its findings. Due to the nature that there maybe several functions active within the Lodge, it is within the discretion of the Master of the Lodge to appoint separate committees for each activity as to not over task one individual committee.

These subcommittees of the Bluehouse Lodge serve important roles in the day to day functions and operations of the Lodge. The primary advantage of them is that it does not take the entire Lodge to act on a matter of interest.

POWERS of SUBORDINATE LODGES

SEC. 1-1   CHARTER

Every subordinate lodge in this jurisdiction must hold a charter from the Grand Lodge or a dispensation issued by authority of its law; and a chartered lodge shall not proceed to work until it shall have been regularly constituted and its officers installed.

SEC. 1-2   SUBORDINATE LODGES POWERS

Subordinate lodges, whether under dispensation or chartered, shall have such powers, and only such powers, as are conferred upon them by the Constitution, Regulations, laws, edicts, and decisions of the Grand Lodge.

SEC. 1-3   CONFER THE DEGREES

Subordinate lodges, and not the Grand Lodge, shall confer the degrees. they are authorized to confer the degrees of Entered Apprentice, Fellow Craft, and Master Mason only. The degrees shall be conferred only in the order named.

SEC. 1-4   RULES AND REGULATIONS

The Grand Lodge shall prescribe rules and regulations for the organization and government of subordinate lodges.

SEC. 1-5   LODGE PRECEDENCE

Lodges shall take precedence according to the dates of their respective charters.

SEC. 1-6   INCORPORATED SUBORDINATE LODGE

No subordinate lodge of the Grand Lodge shall hereafter incorporate under the civil law unless its petitions for such incorporation, together with copies of the proposed charter and by-laws, is filed with the Grand Secretary and is first considered and reported on by the Committee on Masonic Jurisprudence, and is thereafter approved by a two-thirds majority vote of the members present at an annual communication of the Grand Lodge such incorporation of a subordinate lodge shall not in any manner affect, change, or modify its relation with the Grand Lodge. A subordinate lodge, although incorporated prior to the adoption of this CODE, is in all respects subject to the laws of the Grand Lodge notwithstanding its incorporation.

SEC. 1-7   MEMBERS HAVE NO PROPERTY INTEREST

No member of a subordinate lodge shall have any property interest either in his membership in the lodge or in any property which the lodge has acquired or may acquire that can be enforced in law whether or not the lodge has been incorporated under the civil law prior to the adoption of this CODE.

SEC. 1-8   DEBTS

The Grand Lodge is in no manner whatever responsible for the debts and obligations of its subordinate lodges (unincorporated), but it may provide that available assets of a subordinate lodge shall be applied to the payments of such debts and obligations.

CHAPTER 6

The Lodge Planning Process

"GETTING THE JOB DONE"

BLUE LODGE PLANNING PROCESS

Establishing Goals and Objectives

No organization, either fraternal or private, can be successful, in the long term, without establishing well defined goals and objectives from which to direct the membership. Successful goals are those which are conceived with the participation of the membership and executed with their support. Human nature dictates that a person will strive to achieve a goal if it is well defined, understood and accepted. He will not, however, endeavor to work if he has no idea what the ultimate purpose of his labors are. A Lodge without defined and accepted goals is a Lodge without committed and enthusiastic members.

Establishing goals for your Lodge is a group process which should involve your entire roster. Naturally, some, principally your officers, are more important and should be brought into the process early for their participation, ideas and ultimate support. Others, the sideliners and inactive reserve, should be advised of the results of your labors and their input requested. Thus everyone is aware of the existing problems and the manner in which they are going to be resolved. What we are going to do, when it is going to be done and how it is going to be accomplished.

Start the process of establishing goals for your Lodge by following this simple group process:

A. Assemble your officers and perhaps a few interested sideliners in a suitable meeting place, one that offers relaxation and comfort. Obtain and utilize a large "flip" chart and a handful of colored marking pens. Also provide some suitable refreshments to keep the assembled brethren contented.

B. With one man assigned to the chart, begin by asking each man individually - What in your view is the biggest problem existing within our Lodge? Allowing each participant to list only one response, go around the room and solicit an answer from every individual. Continue around the room numerous times until all perceived problems are listed. Remember that every man is different and each has an individual view on what the real problems truly are. Every response must be respected. To ridicule someone's view will effectively remove him from the process and insure his ultimate opposition.

C. Once all the problems are listed, then the group should review the work accomplished and begin to list them in priority. Once completed, you now have a listing of the perceived problems within your Lodge. Some problems will be minor and can be easily resolved by an immediate decision. Others will be major and require extensive plans and work to be achieved.

D. The solutions to these listed problems should be the foundation for the ultimate goals which the leadership of your Lodge should establish. Allow your group to renew the problems and establish a few achievable goals, both short term and long term. Then communicate your goals and plans of action to the membership for their input and ultimate acceptance.

E. Stay on track, continue communicating your goals, and announce all progress and/or problems that you have encountered. What have you just accomplished? Think for a moment. You have begun team building, communicated through a group process, outlined what needs to be accomplished and achieved a "buy in" from both the present and future leadership and the membership. Everyone now knows, in writing, what direction that you and the future Masters of your Lodge are traveling. Additionally, they are aware of what is going to be required of them to accomplish the tasks at hand. The following is just one example of setting proper goals and objectives for your Lodge...

During your meetings, you and your team have concluded that the financial base for your Lodge has been eroded over the past few years and the team has determined that something must be done to correct this deficiency. Therefore, as a group, you have set the following as a goal: Increase the Financial Resources of the Lodge by a specific amount within an established period.

Objectives

The purpose of this element is to simply define and determine exactly what the lodge intends to achieve. It should be clear and concise and above all, <u>realistic</u>.

A. Review present spending to insure that all funds are now being utilized efficiently.

B. Review the historical pattern of spending and savings to ascertain how you arrived at your present levels.

C. Review all sources of income into your Lodge - dues, donations, rentals (use of dining hall), dinners, social events, candidate fees, etc., each as a percentage of total income.

D. Determine what present spending can be reduced to assist in achieving the goal.

E. Determine what fees can be raised and to what levels to achieve the goal.

F. Communicate the findings of your team to the membership through the trestle board, special newsletters and at all meetings.

G. Develop a legitimate plan of action with specific time frames for implementation of all fee increases and/or spending decreases that will meet the goal that your team has set.

H. Bring the goals and objectives before the Lodge for full discussion and approval by a vote of the membership. The work of your team is now an official goal of the Lodge, fully approved, and awaiting implementation.

I. Continually review the plan of action and update it as the need arises to make sure that you and the future leaders are meeting the established goals of your Lodge.

The above is only an example of many such goals and objectives which your Lodge may wish to adopt. The important lesson to be learned is that your Lodge and its membership require specific direction for the Lodge to be productive and the concerns of the membership are addressed and acted on.

Planning

The magnificent Temple that was constructed by King Solomon was not accomplished without detailed and concise plans which outlined all the tasks that were required, when they were to be constructed and who was to do the work. Proper planning leads to concise execution and results in superior performance and ultimately a spirited accomplishment. It is mandatory that you need to establish an overall extensive plan for your year that includes separate detailed plans for each of your term's activities and programs.

The planning process may be thought by some to be unnecessary and a waste of time. However, it is a short sighted view which, in many cases, will result in a severe decline in the quality of "customer service" provided within a Lodge. There are all sorts of plans: some are short term which may relate to a program for a specific evening, and others are long term which may extend over a period of years. The important issue for you to be concerned with is that you and your Lodge have specific plans for every activity and every improvement that is desired, both short and long term. Team building and establishing goals and objectives as outlined above are the beginning of the planning process. You now have the officers and the Lodge communicating with one another for the purpose of improving your Lodge. Now you must begin the process of preparing plans for implementation.

Prior to embarking upon any task, you first must know where you are. Then and only then can you plan which roads you must take and which vehicle you must ride to get you to your desired destination. It is easy to meet, discuss problems and then establish some goals and objectives. The hard part is to actively put them into effect. You can talk all day about the trip you are going to take. The difficulty comes when you must decide where to go, how you're going to get there and how much it is going to cost you. The results of the "problem sharing" and "goal setting" meetings that you have held with your officers and members is the point of departure for the planning process.

Direction

Direction is more than setting your goals and objectives or developing extensive plans. Direction combines the above with specific guidance on completing assigned tasks or overseeing the work. Taking into consideration our present society and the fact that a Lodge is an assembly of volunteers, care must be taken in the manner in which direction is given. It is easy to bark orders in an authoritarian manner. However, little will be accomplished because your membership will soon return to their homes and find something else entertaining to do. Additionally the absence of direction will create a leadership vacuum and absolutely nothing will be accomplished.

Each task within a Lodge requires proper direction if the job is to be completed according to plan. When assigning a task to a member tell him in polite terms what you wish accomplished. Request his input,, decide what path to take and strike an agreement as to what is going to be done. If a disagreement arises regarding the process, praise him for his ideas but then inform him of the manner in which you would like the task to be completed. Use words such as "That is a great idea but if you don't mind I would really like it done this way". In every instance when giving direction, think about the best way to approach a Brother and ultimately obtain his support. Common courtesy and good manners is the "honey that attracts those worker bees".

Direction can also come through a detailed explanation of what the requirements are for each job within a Lodge. Did you give your officers and Committee chairmen a job description of their duties and responsibilities? Verbal descriptions often times are insufficient to provide adequate direction. Call a meeting with your team and completely review each task within the Lodge and assign it to an individual.

The Section on duties of Blue Lodge Officers on pages 119 - 128 of this Handbook has an excellent description of the duties and responsibilities for these officers and committees. Use them where appropriate or change them to reflect the traditions of your Lodge, but above all, commit the routine and required duties of each officer and committee member to writing. Finally, distribute the materials to those involved and make sure that they understand what is required of them.

THE BLUE LODGE TRESTLEBOARD

The METHOD to the madness

How often have we ever ask the question or heard someone say… What's going on in the Lodge? When is the next meeting or even what type of meeting are we having tonight?… Sounds familiar? These and similar questions floods the scene time and time again. We (the Lodge) can reduce this effect by improving the flow of communication between our members by developing a practical avenue of communication. We (the membership) must do our part by putting forth an effort of receiving and acting upon the information generated.

The BlueLodge is a well established and organized society, not unlike any other and the way that an organized and structured organization operates, this point can never be stressed enough. What makes us different is our procedures and protocols, having said this, the flow of information remains as vital to the operation of the Lodge as any other.

The Masonic Trestleboard is the planned calendar that is developed and posted from the highest level in the Masonic chain, the Grand Lodge, down to each and all constituent Lodges. It Describes all events that has been planned for that organization that posted it.

It is imperative that well governed organization of our fraternity employ the use of this tool. Conceive this notion? *Where are we and where are we going! Or What have we done and what is there to do!* To some this is something perhaps we have heard before, on the other hand to the masses, it is lingering in the their minds, its meaning. The preceding statement is really not a condescending one, but a significant one to describe the truth of not understanding the Trestleboard, but the need for Masonic Education and Training in respect to it.

The DEGREE ELEMENT

Masters, Wardens and all those members serving on committees must apply methodical and practical approaches to the establishment and development of the Trestleboard. This is the **MASTER PLAN** of the Lodge. Factors to consider for this process, however not limited to are;

1. **D**etermine what is in the Budget and the direction the Lodge intends to proceed in.
2. **E**stablish goals that are realistic and within arms reach.
3. **G**et creative in developing ways to finance and build capital for Lodge ventures.
4. **R**estore enthusiasm in sidelined members.
5. **E**mploy the services of outside sources.
6. **E**stablished a well developed plan to this approach.

Now, the flipside of the Trestleboard is that it is not just an event calendar, it is the spirit that drives each member of the Lodge, it plants in each member the purpose for his membership and the mission that he and his fellow brethren are to accomplish, it explains the meaning for actions and reactions of his performance and contribution. It highlights to the public the positive nature of this fraternal organization, that our existence being for the better good of the community at large.

Design and format of your Trestleboard does not matter, the important thing here is that the information presented on or in the trestleboard is clear, meaning; its stating the information clearly, not to be misunderstood by whomever reads it. It should at least state the description of the event, time and location.

Sample
UNITY LODGE No. 21
F. & A. M.
Calendar and Event Schedule
Masonic Year 2000-2001
(TRESTLE BOARD)

EVENT	DATE
Fund Raiser (Independence Day Rib Fest)	July 4, 2000
Officers/Budget Committee meeting	July 12, 2000
Regular Communication	July 26, 2000
Business meeting	August 9, 2000
(Proposal of Master's Banquet)	
Fund Raiser (Bowling Challenge)	August 11, 2000
Regular Communication	August 26, 2000
Youth Council meeting (Senior Advisors)	September 10, 2000
Regular Communication (cancelled)	September 27, 2000
Com. service visitation - Children's Hospital	September 30, 2000
District Conference	October 9, 2000
Business meeting (cancelled)	October 9, 2000
Regular Communication	October 24, 2000
(Raffle drawing)	
Youth Council campout	Oct 31– Nov 1, 2000
Business meeting	November 6, 2000
Youth Council meeting (Senior Advisors)	November 8, 2000
Regular Communication	November 22, 2000
Fund Raiser (Master's Banquet)	November 29, 2000
Black Month (No Masonic Business)	
St. Johns Day Recognition (MM only)	December 19, 2000

Business meeting	January 8, 2001
Youth Council meeting (Senior Advisors)	January 10, 2001
Leadership Workshop	January 24-25, 2001
(District Lodge of Instruction)	
Regular Communication (cancelled)	January 24, 2001
Business meeting	February 12, 2001
Fund Raiser (Sweetheart's Ball)	February 14, 2001
Regular Communication	February 28, 2001
Com. Service – 5th St. Clean-up	March 11, 2001
Business meeting (cancelled)	March 11, 2001
Regular Communication	March 27, 2001
Youth Council meeting (Sr. Advisors)	April 3, 2001
Com. Service (Annual Easter Egg Hunt)	Easter Sunday
Business Meeting	April 8, 2001
Regular Communication (cancelled)	April 24, 2001
District Raising	April 24, 2001
Lodge Study Session	May 6, 2001
Regular Communication	May 22, 2001
(Lodge books prepared for Annual audit)	
Business meeting (Annual Election)	June 5, 2001
Youth Council Activity (Flag Day)	June 14, 2001
Regular Communication (cancelled)	June 19, 2001
MWGL 2004 Annual Session	June 19-23, 2001

NOTE: Start time for all Business meetings are 6:30 pm promptly
Start time for all Regular Communications are 3:00 pm promptly.

A. KEITH JONES

DRESS: Business meetings dress is B/W

Regular Communications are casual (dark slacks, polo shirt)

*NOTE: Schedule subject to change due to conflicting events and member commitments

CONSTITUENT LODGE ADMINISTRATION

Before we can explore these views, we must be first familiar with some of the terms used;

AGENT: A person acting or doing business for another.

AFTER-ACTION REPORT: A report outlining the concluded result(s) of an activity or event.

ASSESSMENT: An imposed rate or amount (as a tax) for a specific cause or use.

BUDGET: A financial report containing estimates of income and expenses; also a plan for coordinating income and expenses.

DUES: Fees paid for continued membership.

EXPENDITURE: The act or process of expending; actual paid amount for service or merchandise.

EXPENSE: The cause of an expenditure; the actual cost for an expenditure.

FIDUCIARY: The invoked trust or confidence; held in trust for another.

INCOME: Monetary gain(s) derived from labor, services, business or property.

INVESTMENT: The outlay of money for income or profit.

PRELIMINARY REPORT: A report outlining the estimated cost for an activity or event.

PRINCIPLE: The person(s) from whom the agent's authority derives.

RECAPITULATION: To restate briefly or summarize.

RESERVES: Moneys held back for future or specific use.

Factors that should influence the process of the Lodge accounting is the Who, What, When, Where, Why and How, however not limited to, are as follows;

*__Who__ is responsible for the execution of the Lodge Budget.

1. The Worshipful Master, Wardens and Members of the Finance Committee.

2. All Members on the active roll should be involved in its development.

*__What__ is the most important document in regards to Lodge finances.

1. The Budget; as previous defined, the Worshipful Master presents the budget for the ensuing year to be voted on and adopted by members of the Lodge.

2. The budget is developed based on the prospected goals envisioned by the Worshipful Master as presented to the Lodge at the beginning of the year.

3. Disbursements to the Grand Lodge are considered before those of the Lodge.

*__When__ are the plans for the budget presented and approved by the Lodge. 1. At the earliest time possible after election and installation of the new Officers.

*__Where__ is the planning and decisions of the Lodge finances taken place. 1. All official Business of administration and finance are in Open Lodge.

*__Why__ is the specific reason for the cause of an activity. It simply states the "purpose"

*__How__ indicates the procedural process or dissemination relative to a specific activity.

NOTE: Why and How are further expanded in the section covering Lodge Finance on page 143.

Administrative Responsibilities

t is the overall responsibility of every Worshipful Master to ensure that the administrative process of his Lodge is carried out properly.. Furthermore, he is also to ensure that his duties are carried out within the policies and protocols of Grand Lodge procedures, of which jurisdiction the Lodge serving authority. The primary purpose of this is to ensure that Lodges within that jurisdiction are operating consistently with these processes. Such operations and activities include, however not limited to are:

*General Administration

*Handling Petitions

*Proper recordings of Minutes

*Budget and Finance

*Proper recordings of General Receipts and Disbursements

*Completing Semi and Annual Returns

*Forwarding scheduled reports to the Grand Lodge

General Administration

This function represents one of the most vital areas of Lodge operations, no Lodge can operate sufficiently without control and attentive record keeping. This holds true for all aspects of Lodge operations. The office of Lodge Secretary outside that of the Master, is most critical to the success and smooth flow of actions and activities of the Lodge. The Lodge Secretary is the only member in the Lodge that has his hands on all that goes on in the Lodge, outside of the Master, he has direct knowledge of what is in the records, the Lodge financial status, old business, new business, basically the WHO, WHAT, WHEN, WHERE and HOW. This should be well considered at election time when selecting and choosing this worthy brother, because the job he undertakes does not end at the closing of the Lodge. The reality is, as most longtime members will attest is that the duties and responsibilities of this office begins and end only at election time, at the point of his installation. To generalize his basic duties, in no particular sequence and not limited to;

1. Receives All monies that comes into the Lodge, and those that are disbursed from the Lodge shall be recorded, to include who it came from, description of the transaction, date of transaction and type of transaction, for disbursements, identification of the recipient(s).

2. All financial transaction within the Lodge shall be substantiated by receipt.

3. Each financial member shall have a current Dues card with the proper annotation of the secretary. A log or record of dues maintained on each member of his financial status.

4. Member records shall consist of all vital information on each member. This is the only way that the Lodge can account for its membership. To include current mailing address and all beneficiary information.

5. Each member of the Lodge shall affix his signature to the log in affirmation of his acknowledgement and receipt of the Lodge Constitution and By-Laws.

6. Proper recording of the proceedings (minutes) of each communication shall be maintained, to be archived as a historical record should future actions require its recall.

The items listed below are additional administrative requirements of Lodges for the purpose of Grand Lodge reporting;

1. Current Memorial Fund registry card: Each financial member shall have a completed card forwarded to the Grand Lodge for eligibility for his benefactors to this fund.

2. The Secretary shall compile a report , from the records and report the same as a quarterly report of the Lodge member status, accompanied with the proper fees and assessments, to the Grand Lodge at scheduled period. The same to be made annually.

3. The Secretary shall compile a report, from the records and report the same as certificate of the Lodge credential for validation of its voting status at the annual session.

Handling Petitions

Generally, as with all administrative procedures, each Grand Lodge has its own particular procedure for the disposition of petitions within its jurisdiction, each Lodge should follow the administrative procedure as outlined by the Grand Lodge to ensure consistency as well as proper protocol. These protocols shall include, however not limited to;

1. Accountability - That information presented on the petition remain uncompromised by being exposed to outside or public influences. This also includes the that the proper application of the application, meaning that the information on the petition is correct and truthful, this responsibility initially lies with the Lodge member who passes out the petition and vouches for the candidate.

2. Security - That the body and content of information provided by its profanes are not violated or carelessly unprotected by its caretakers (the craft). Each Lodge has the responsibility for the safeguard of petitions, whether it is completed by a candidate or not.

3. Process - That procedural and proper actions are taken on the petition. Proper ballet made on the petition, accepted or not, handed back over to the secretary for the proper annotations and archiving.

Lodge Ritualistic Works

• As a general practice, the Ritualistic works of Lodges are usually consistent throughout the jurisdiction, with all Lodges of that jurisdiction using the same published Ritual. However, proficiency of new members of Lodges maybe different than that of one Lodge to the next. With each Lodge having at its disposal one(1) or more Past Masters, as well as the Senior Warden, Lodges performing Ritualistic works should never find itself stumbling through it especially when it comes to performing degree work. If necessary, the Master should schedule rehearsals sessions to ensure when time comes for the Lodge to do Degree work, the officers know their part. It is embarrassing to the entire Lodge when its officers can't or don't work through the Ritual properly when they bring in new membership. Study sessions are vital to the Lodge, it is the responsibility of each member to help each other, new members don't learn who or what we are unless the experience ones enlighten them. One Master may organize the study sessions of his Lodge different from another. The bottom line is that we must know what we're talking about and what we're doing before we say it or do it in the Lodge. **" Better to be ignorant of a matter than to know half of it"**, this quote, if understood will keep us out of trouble.

• Another issue is the practice of Masonic usages. These not only vary with Lodges but with jurisdictions as a whole. An examples of this is; 3-5-7, walking the Tyler's sword, working your way in, all these are elements of the works of the Masonic conscience, they are taught by the experience members of Lodges to the uninformed Brothers. It is the responsibility of the Master, whether delegated to some other member or committee or not, that the members of his Lodge is informed of Masonic usages and practices. Masonic Education falls on the shoulders of the Master and Past Masters of the Lodge.

Lodge Budget and Finance

In general, it goes without saying and without any question, this area represents the most critical of any Lodge activity. No organization can sustain itself without the proper systematic approach to its accounting operation. Size does not matter, Lodges with as few as 3-5 members to Lodges having the membership 50 or more, the application of good financial record keeping remains the same in all respect. This manual does not represent every element that exist in the functions of Lodge finance operations or the direct protocol or procedures directed or required by any specific Grand Lodge, only generalized procedures as seen by the author of this material. Another factor to consider is, in order to create a budget that all members can relate to, is to ensure that the budget report reflects those activities items in the Tretsleboard that has been accepted by members of the Lodge, and they are represented in the Budget. Remember, approval of the budget require 2/3rd vote or a majority of the members present, whichever the case may be in accordance with what and how its outline in the Lodge By-Laws. Other factors to consider, however not limited to are;

*__Why__ is the budget so important to the Lodge?

1. It places the Lodge on a correct path for positive productivity and growth.

2. It keeps the Lodge aware of limitations.

*__How__, by establishing procedures of operations;

1. All general receipts are received by the Secretary.

2. Proper recording of the receipts is crucial.

3. The Secretary must make correct notations as to accounts, that each payment made by members and other sources receive the proper credit.

4. All moneys received and accounted for by the Secretary, gets handed over to the Treasurer for proper deposit.

5. It is the responsibility of the Master to ensure that all schedule financial report are properly completed for presentation to the Lodge.

A) Payments of assessments are always considered for credit before dues.

B) The Secretary is to ensure that a receipt is given for all payments made.

C) Develop Preliminary reports when planning fund raisers or events.

D) Develop After-Action reports at the conclusion of events.

** The membership are the principles, the officers are the agents

**It is the Fiduciary responsibility of the agents
to act in the best interest of the Lodge!**

THE BUDGET

In review, the Budget is an estimate of all income and expenses, its capital gains of the Lodge during a specific Masonic year. This includes income and expenses from administrative or operating activities or any other source that effects its accounting throughout the Masonic year. The bottom line is, anything that comes in or goes out, or is to be, should at least be addressed in the Budget. The whole motivational factor here is the accountability of the officers of this committee having "FORESIGHT" in developing an effective scheme in producing a concise and realistic Budget.

Influences on the Budget

(Which came first, the chicken or the egg?)

Simply stating, Influences on the budget refers to what goals your Lodge establishes and wish to accomplish. This is an important element in developing an effective "**scheme**", and for the most part, serves as the primary purpose for the development of the budget. In order for any of these to hold water, your Lodge first must have **PURPOSE**.

Several factors must be considered, these factors are also influenced by other elements in the overall planning process. While developing the budget, Lodge officers must have the presence of mind, the direction in which to progress the Lodge, not confusing this with the goals that has been establish, which relates to the objectives. "**Direction**" refers to the management of that process.

Throughout the process, the officers will become aware that accomplish one thing, something else has to be completed or at least accomplished at the same time. Example, how can a budget be completed if we don't know what activities the Lodge is to support? Or What activities can the Lodge plan if we don't know what funds are available to allocate for that event? Well the answer to these questions is knowing what PURPOSE the Lodge is serving and understanding the Direction you intend to get there. With Lodge leaders and members working together on the several committees, can find solutions to support the endeavors of the Lodge.

The Committees (Events/Activities)

Upon completion of the Trestleboard, the members of this committee should give it a final review to analyze the overall plan to ensure that it is well balanced and offers a good variety of activities and programs for all members. The overall objective in the whole scheme of things is for each and every member of the Lodge contributing to the process of the Lodge business, do so with the best interest of the Lodge foremost in mind. Consider these factors;

1. Are the activities in the tresleboard appropriate for the Lodge current situation, are the objectives outlined logically (membership, resources and the budget)?

2. Are the activities varied and dispersed throughout the term evenly and well balanced?

3. Does the trestleboard as a whole represent the interest of all Lodge members? And finally;

4. Can the Lodge afford it, and how do we pay for it?

Preparing the Budget

The last question mentioned above may seem to some, mark the beginning or the end to this process. It leads us to believe that we should just start the process over, how could we have a budget and no planned trestleboard or how can we have a trestleboard and no planned budget? Well the answer is that you can not have one with out the other. The Trestleboard tends to reflect the ideas of the members of the Lodge for the activities and events. The Budget on the other hand reflect the ways and means of supporting those ideas.

It would be irresponsible for the committee on Budget and Finance to only consider the fixed income of the Lodge to support its ventures. Lodges must create creative approaches to gain or increase their capital base by having fund raising events, and within the plan it must also consider and establish long range goals to support the longevity of the Lodge for its future growth by investing and paying itself first and foremost. By doing this, it will place the Lodge in a position where it is self sufficient, not having to rely on just the membership dues for its financial sovereignty.

In evaluating the budget, compare the expenditures against the income to determine where the weak areas are, this gives you a starting point. From the Trestleboard, events planned that require funding beyond the limits of current balances or estimated cost for those events that may cause the balance to go in the negative, try not to cancel them or put them off due to funding, but rather consider more economical ways of funding them. The object is to cover all expenses during the term of the Masonic year and to build capital for the future financial stability of the Lodge. Elements that should be considered;

1. Determine the current total balances that are available.

2. Determine the total cost for the term (Masonic Year).

3. Determine the total cost for each activity, month by month.

4. Determine and list all fixed expenses on a monthly basis.

5. Analyze and evaluate all of your fixed income, by activity on a monthly basis.

6. Analyze and evaluate the investment income and interest applied.

7. Review and balance your budget.

8. Prepare it for distribution to all Lodge members, so that everyone has a part in the process of its development and is also responsible for its conception.

Description of Items in a Budget

1. Operating Expenses

    a). Masonic Hall/Building

    b). Utilities

    c). Lodge supplies

    d). Misc. (postage/printing)

2. Events/Activities Expenses

   a). Grand Lodge fees and taxes

   b). Fund Raising events expenses

   c). Fraternal Assistance/Charity

   d). Grand Lodge Memorial Fund

3. Receipts and Income

   a). Membership fees and dues

   b). Fund Raising events revenue

   c). Interest from investment accounts

   d). Donations

   e). Lodge Charity Fund

4. Recapitulation – Adjustment of expenses and income and review of the items totaled that make-up total amounts for specific funds in the budget report.

5. Summary - Totals for all categories in the main body of the budget to derive total net of capital gains.

Sample
Unity Lodge No. 21
Budget Report
Masonic Year 2000-2001

July 15, 2000

DEBIT		CREDIT
Special Funds (as of July 1, 2000)	$5190.00	
Beginning Balance	$1000.00	
Projected Operating Expenses		
1. Masonic Hall	$360.00	
2. Lodge Supplies	250.00	
3. Misc.	100.00	
Projected Events/ Activity		
1. Grand Lodge Taxes	$700.00	
2. Grand Lodge Mem. Fund	200.00	
3. Lodge Fraternal Assistance	500.00	
4. High-Noon Carwash	150.00	500.00
5. Past Master's Night	500.00	1800.00
6. Master's Charity Banquet	1350.00	2500.00
7. Bowling Night	50.00	100.00
8. Youth Activity Donation	150.00	
9. District Conference	150.00	
10. Charity Donation	500.00	
11. Lodge Hall Htg. Unit	1200.00	
12. Membership Fees (new)		570.00
13. Membership Dues		1440.00

14. Investment Interest   60.00

15. Lodge Charity Account   500.00

    Total Income/Expenses $6160.00 $13,660.00

RECAPITULATION

Expense	$ 6,160.00	
Income	$13,660.00	
Adjusted Balance (Total Income)		$7500.00
Special Funds (Remittance)	$ 5,190.00	
Adjusted Balance (General Account)		$2310.00

Special Funds

Investment Account (EE Bonds)	{$ 2500.00}	$2,000.00
(1 ea. $1000.00 Cert. Per year @ $500.00 / 1995-2000)		$1,000.00
Lodge Charity Account		$ 500.00
Lodge Benevolence Fund		$2,625.00
Lodge Building Fund		$1,500.00
Adj. Total Special Funds		$7,625.00
Capital Gains	$2,435.00	

SUMMARY

Balance (General Account)	$2,310.00
Special Funds	7,625.00
Net Totals (all Accounts)	$ 9,935.00

Preparing Reports

One of the actions that any and every productive Lodge implements as we now acknowledge, is having managerial control of itself.... Now what do we mean by this, well its very simple. In a nut shell, all it is, is having all your ducks in the proverbial row, knowing where the Lodge stands administratively and financially at any given time. This should be a matter simply of just going to the records.

This brings us to the question of; What are the reports that are vital to managerial control? It begins with the conception of having an application or petition on file for every member of the Lodge, past and present. This marks the beginning of the historical records of the membership of the Lodge. To always remain as part of the archives of the Lodge.

The task of maintaining reports and record keeping is not as much a difficult job as it seem, as long as those items being reported are kept current in the scheme of things, meaning anything that requires logging or annotating are logged and annotated, having done so, a formal record of report can be accomplished. Types of reports include, however not limited to are;

1. Quarterly, semi-annual and annual returns.
2. Budget reports.
3. Special committee reports.
4. Preliminary and after action event reports. (to be further explain later in this chapter)
5. Financial statements and reports.

These reports do take some time to prepare, however they do serve a legitimate purpose. Imagine this; Its at the end of the Masonic year, election are about to take place, but the Lodge has not turned over the books to the audit team designated by the Grand Lodge. The Lodge held a fund raiser toward the end of the year that has not been disposed of by the Lodge and reported in the minutes and financial records. Even though this fund raiser was a success for the Lodge with a substantial net profit, it does not matter, these fund require formal report to be made and recorded to reflect the entire financial balance for the Masonic year. Otherwise the audit team can not conduct an accurate review of the Treasury books. This is but one example of the crucial ness why it is important to maintain up to date records.

Events and Activities Report

A large amount of Lodge revenue is generated through Events and Activities such as fund raisers, at the very conception of this activity, it becomes a financial issue for the Lodge and therefore, serious attention must be given to the nature of it. For the most part, there is no specific protocol as to procedure that has been established by Grand bodies for Lodges to carryout such activities, only that they represent and reflect the good will of the craft, some Grand Bodies do indeed have such protocol of procedures and enforce the with a firm hand to ensure compliance. Be this as it may, some don't and therefore, this section may be a helpful consideration in applying such protocol.

At the time it is addressed and requested in opened Lodge for an event or activity to take place, several action take effect, mainly what is it going to cost the Lodge to conduct such an activity, after the recommendation has been made in the form of a favorable vote taken to send it to the committee for initial planning, it becomes the responsibility of that committee to determine whether or not it is feasible for the Lodge to conduct such activity. Applying what ever methods and gathering all necessary information to draw its conclusions, be they what they may, the committee should analyze the best course of action for the event to be a success. Part of conducting a thorough planning process is to conduct a financial plan, a Preliminary Financial Report to present to the Lodge once all they arrive at a conclusion. This report will give all members a clear understanding of what to expect if final vote is reached to move forward with the event.

The following is an example of such an event and Preliminary Financial Report;

It has been recommended by the Senior Warden that Unity Lodge begin the planning of its annual Master's Charity Banquet, the Lodge votes to send the recommendation to the Events Committee. The committee's initial review indicates that during past years, the cost for the banquet has been around $3000.00 and the current year's budget and general account balance can support this amount for this years banquet. Again, the whole idea is to show what the expected initial cost may be. There is always the chance that items can be eliminated or even added on to the list of expenditures or even the income, be this as it may, the lodge does not go into the venture blindly. This is what, at all cost, you want to avoid. When it comes to money and finance, your Lodge should conduct these matters as a "business".

(The following Preliminary Financial report on the next page is generic in form, its sole purpose is to show an itemized estimated cost of the banquet so that the budget for the event is not exceeded.)

Sample
Unity Lodge No. 21
Preliminary Financial Report
Master's Charity Banquet

August 20, 2000

SUBJECT: Preliminary Financial projection

Master's Charity Banquet Fund Raiser

TO: Wor. Master, Wardens and Brethren of Unity Lodge No. 21

1. The following is a preliminary financial projection of the proposed up-coming annual fund Raising event, Master's Charity Banquet and Scholarship Campaign.

2. All figures indicated are projections of the total cost to the Lodge for the proposed Fund raising event November 27, 2000.The overall budget for the event is set at $3000.00 The following projected figures are subject to change due to Increasing economic factors.

I. Projections as follows;

Income:

a). Member Assessment $30.00
25 @ $30 ....$ 750.00
b). Ticket sales (8 to each member/total of 200 tickets)
200 @ $15 per ticket $3000.00
c). Annual Donation (Pepsi-Cola, City Council)................$1500.00
Total direct projected income $5250.00

II. Expenditures:

a). Masonic Hall.. $150.00

(clean-up crew)

b). Catering Fees $700.00

c). Entertainment $150.00

d). Guest Speaker Donation .... $ 50.00

e). Total Donations Disp. $2500.00

Total projected expenditures $3550.00

III. Recapitulation:

Total projected income $5250.00

Total projected expenditures...................$3550.00

Total projected net profit $1700.00

4. The Lodge will incur an additional $50.00 for guest speaker.

5. The expenditure section indicates an amount exceeding the authorized budget, however this amount is off-set by annual donations from City Council and Pepsi-Cola.

5. Selected committee shall submit final cost projections at the scheduled communication in October.

FRATERNALLY Submitted,

After-Action or Post Financial Report (Final)

Upon completion of the event, the same committee has the responsibility of compiling all the information pertaining to the event, and presenting the results of their finding to the Lodge. This should be in the form of a similar report as that of a Preliminary report called an After-Action or Post Financial Report. Remember the Preliminary report described all estimated costs, the A-Action or Post report describes all **"actual"** cost expenses and receipts, it is the final report that closes out any and all actions pertaining to the event or activity it addresses. The structure of the report is the same as the prelim. The difference is that all figures and amounts indicate the actual monies paid out by the lodge for the items descriptions.

Sample
Unity Lodge No. 21
Financial Report (Final)
Master's Charity Banquet

December 5, 2000

SUBJECT: Financial Report (AAR) Master's Charity Banquet
Fund Raiser

TO: Wor. Master, Wardens and Brethren of Unity Lodge No. 21

1. The following is a final financial report of the annual fund Raising event, Master's Charity Banquet and Scholarship Campaign.

2. All figures indicate the actual total cost of income and expenditures to the Lodge for the Fund raising event held on November 27, 2000. The overall budget for the event was set at $3000.00.

I. <u>INCOME</u>:

a). Member Assessment $30.00
    25 @ $30 .... $ 750.00
b). Ticket sales (8 to each member/total of 200 tickets)
    200 @ $15 per ticket $3000.00
c). Annual Corporate Donation (Pepsi-Cola Co., $1500.00 /
    City Council, $500.00) $2000.00
Total direct projected income $5750.00

II. <u>EXPENDITURES</u>:

    a). Masonic Hall $250.00
    (clean-up crew)
    b). Catering Fees $800.00

c). Entertainment $150.00

d). Guest Speaker Donation $100.00

e). Total Donations Disp. $2500.00

Total projected expenditures $3800.00

III. Recapitulation:

Total Income $5750.00

Total Expenditures $3800.00

Total projected net profit $1950.00

4. The Lodge incurred an additional $50.00 for guest speaker.

5. The expenditure section indicates an amount exceeding the authorized budget, however this amount is off-set by increased annual donations from City Council and Pepsi-Cola Bottling Co.

6. The expenditure section indicates an increase in the charges for \Masonic Hall clean-up and Catering fees.

7. The overall report reflects a positive increase of profit made by the event.

FRATERNALLY Submitted,

ADMINISTRATIVE FORMS
USED BY LODGES

1. MEMBER LEDGER SHEET (L)- Form used to notate and archive general and historical information on each member of the Lodge. It serves as the official "Authenticated record" of data of its members. Each member is to have a Ledger Sheet prepared upon the order of the Wor. Master upon initiation.

2. MEMORIAL FUND card (GL)- Death benefit certificate for each member of a constituent Lodge, all members must have this card completed and on file with the Grand Secretary for entitlement of this fund. (may not be required in all jurisdictions)

3. MEMBER DUES card (GL)- Official membership card to signify a members financial and current membership status.

4. LODGE CREDENTIAL Form (GL)- Form used in the Grand Lodge to validate a Lodge's voting status.

5. ANNUAL RETURN Sheet (GL)- Form used in the Grand Lodge by each Lodge to complete for the purpose financial accountability. (Quarterly, Semi and Annual report for the same purpose).

6. MEMBERSHIP APPLICATION (GL)- Form used for all petitioners of a jurisdiction for membership.

7. APPLICATION for AFFILIATION (L)- Form used for all members applying for affiliation in a particular local Lodge, retaining membership in his Home Lodge, accompanied with a current Dues card and/or Demit.

8. APPLICATION for DEMIT (L)- Form used for all members applying for membership from another Lodge or jurisdiction, being financial, from which the Lodge issuing the Demit.

*NOTE: Some jurisdiction may require additional administration forms.

GLOSSARY

A

ABIF: Meaning is "his father".

ADONAI: The lord.

ADVANCE: Going from one degree to the next after showing proficiency in the preceding degree.

ADVERSE BALLOT: In case the ballot on a petition for the degrees or for affiliation is adverse, the Master may, if he so desires, spread the ballot again to make certain no error occurred. In so doing, he should state his reason for the second spreading. The ballot shall not be spread a third time.

A.A.O.N.M.S: Ancient Arabic Order Nobles Mystic Shrine

A.E.A.O.N.M.S.: Ancient Egyptian Arabic Order Nobles Mystic Shrine

AGREEABLY: In conformity with.

ALLEGORICAL: An allegory is a story told through symbols, or an idea so expressed.

ALLEGORY: Analogy or comparison; a story told to illustrate a principle. It comes from the Greek meaning "to say something different."

ALL SEEING-EYE: An emblem reminding us that we are constantly in God's presence.

ALPHA and OMEGA: First and last Greek letters of the alphabet. The beginning and the end of all things; the first and the last, often mentioned in the Scriptures and in several of the Masonic degrees.

AMEN: From the Hebrew meaning "verily, truly, certainly." One person confirms the words of another. Masonically, answered by "So mote it be."

ANCIENT: Old, time honored.

ANNO BENEFACIO: (A.B.) Latin for "In the Year of the Blessing." Used by the Order of High Priesthood for dating their documents. (1930 added to the current date.)

ANNO DEPOSITIONIS: (A.Dep.) Latin for "In the Year of the Deposit. "The Cryptic Masonic date designation. (Add 1000 to the current date.)

ANNO DOMINI: (A.D.) Latin for "Year of our Lord."

ANNO INVENTIONIS: (A.I.) Latin meaning "In the Year of Discovery." The Royal Arch date designation. (Add 530 to the current date.)

ANNO LUCIS: (A.L.) Latin meaning "In the Year of Light, "the date used by Ancient Craft Masonry. (Add 4000 to the current date.)

ANNO MUNDI: (A.M.) Latin meaning "In the Year of the World." The date used by the Scottish Rite. (Add 3760 to the current year until September; if after September, add 3761.

ANNO ORDINIS: (A.0.) L thin meaning "In the Year of Order." The date used by the Knights Templar. (Subtract 1118 from the current date.)

ANOINT: To apply oil to, or pour oil on, particularly holy oil as a sign of elevation to kingship or consecration to priesthood. Hence, "anointed," one accepted by the Lord, as "The Lord's anointed." . Comes from the custom of the Egyptians and Jews.

APPRENTICE: Comes from the Latin word apprehendre meaning "to grasp, to master a thing." Hence, a learner.

APRON: The badge of a Mason. Originally among priesthoods as a badge of office and a means of ornamentation. The Masonic apron should be white lambskin, fourteen inches wide and twelve inches deep. It should be presented to the candidate at his initiation and not at some subsequent time. No substitute should be used. From the French word napron meaning "an apron of cloth." From earliest times in Persia, Egypt, India, the Jewish Essenes, the white apron was a badge of honor and candidates were invested with it, or a sash, or a robe. Its reference is to purity of heart, to innocence of conduct.

ARCHITECT: One who designs buildings.

ARCHITECTURE: The art or science of building.

ARCHIVES: a place for the safe keeping of records ; the records themselves.

ARTIFICER: a craftsman or skilled laborer.

ARTS: branches of learning, as in the lecture of the F.C. degree. In E.A. degree: skills.

ASHLAR: a block of stone from which a column, capital, or other finished product is carved or hewn.

ASHLAR: A stone as taken from the quarry; an unpolished stone.

ATHEIST: One who does not believe in God.

B

BEEHIVE: Symbolic of systematized industry. What one may not be able to accomplish alone may be easily performed when all work together at one task.

BLAZING STAR: Symbol of light; of Divine direction in the journey through life; symbolizes a true Freemason who, by perfecting himself in the way of truth (knowledge), becomes like a blazing star. In English lodges, symbolizes sun which enlightens the earth, dispensing its blessings to all mankind and giving light and life to all things.

BLUE LODGE. A term which has grown into use over the years meaning the three degrees of the lodge, or Symbolic Masonry. In the early years, Master Masons wore blue lined aprons. Blue is symbolic of perfection, benevolence, truth, universal friendship, fidelity.

BOAZ: Comes from the Hebrew meaning "in strength." The left hand pillar that stood at the porch of King Solomon's Temple.

BOOK OF CONSTITUTIONS: An emblem of law signifying that our moral and spiritual character is grounded in law and order and that no man can live a satisfying life who lives lawlessly.

BOOK OF CONSTITUTIONS GUARDED BY THE TYLER'S SWORD: An admonishment to the Mason that he should be guarded in his words and actions; obedience to the law.

BOOK OF THE LAW: The sacred book which reveals the will of God. To Christians, the Bible; to the Brahman, the Vedas, etc.

BRETHREN: The term is used in speaking of Masons, and in this connection is preferable to "brothers."

BROKEN COLUMN: Columns or pillars were used among the early Hebrews to signify nobles or princes; it is from such that we get the expression "pillar of the church." Masonically, the broken column refers to the fall of one of the chief supporters of the Craft; an untimely death.

C

CLANDESTINE: not regular.

CABLE TOW: The tie by which the candidate is bound to his brethren; the length of a Mason's cable tow is the scope of his ability to go to the relief of a brother in need. In early years the distance was three miles; in present time it is usually considered about forty miles.

CALENDAR, MASONIC: Masons date their official documents in a manner peculiar to themselves. The various dates for the different bodies are based on important points in history.

CANOPY: a tent-like covering. "Canopy of heaven", the sky.

CARDINAL POINTS: East: Wisdom; West: Strength; South: Beauty; North: Darkness.

CARDINAL VIRTUES: Temperance, Fortitude, Prudence, and justice are virtues of morality as laid down by Plato. Cardinal comes from the Latin cardo meaning "chief or fundamental."

CATECHISM: Instructions of Freemasonry.

CEDARS: Members of the Tall Cedars of Lebanon, a non-Masonic organization composed of Freemasons.

CELESTIAL CANOPY: Symbolic covering of the lodge; heavenly.

CEMENT: Brotherly love binds Freemasons of all countries, races and creeds in one common brotherhood.

CHECKERED FLOOR: The Mosaic Pavement.

CHRISTIAN VIRTUES: Faith, Hope, and Charity.

CHALK, CHARCOAL, AND CLAY: Freedom, fervency, and zeal.

CHAPITERS: the ornamental tops or capitals of pillars.

CHARTER: a document setting forth a set of granted rights and privileges given by the Grand Lodge to the constituent Lodge at the time of Constitution. The Master is its custodian, and must see to its security at all times. The charter must be in the Lodge room during all communications of the Lodge, preferably in the Master's charge, but it may be on the Secretary's desk, or in the archives of the Lodge. It should not be framed to hang on the wall. The request of a visitor to inspect the charter in advance be granted or refused. Should the charter be lost or destroyed, the Grand Master or Grand Secretary should be notified at once. Pending the issuing of a duplicate charter, a permission, or dispensation to continue work should be obtained from the Grand Master.

CHASTEN: To correct by discipline.

CIRCLE: A figure which has neither beginning nor end and symbolizes eternity; the universe.

CIRCURNAMBULATION: The movement is in imitation of the apparent course of the sun, and so is in the form of an ellipse. After the obligation the Senior Deacon with the candidate should make all turns square.

CIRCUMSCRIBED: literally encircled hence limited.

CLOTHED, PROPERLY: With white gloves and apron, and the jewel of his Masonic rank. Today the gloves are usually dispensed with.

COLUMNS: From the Latin culmen meaning "a pillar to support or adorn a building." In Masonry the symbolic Significance pertains to the supports of a lodge: Wisdom, Strength and Beauty.

COLUMNS, WARDENS: Represent Jachin and Boaz. While the lodge is at work the columns are erect and horizontal, respectively; while on refreshment, such positions are reversed.

COMMUNICATIONS: The meetings of a Symbolic lodge.

COMPASS: A mathematical instrument for dividing and drawing circles; an instrument indicating the magnetic meridian.

COMPASSES: One of the Working Tools. Freemasons have adopted the plural spelling to distinguish it from the magnetic compass.

CORNICE: The ornamented slab placed above the capital of a pillar, and extending beyond it.

COWANS: profanes, pretenders, intruders, particularly those seeking to obtain the secrets of Masonry unlawfully.

CORNUCOPIA: The horn of plenty; a symbol of abundance.

CORN, WINE, AND OIL: Three elements of consecration. In ancient times these were regarded as the basic commodities for the support of life and constituted the wealth of the people. Today in the U.S. we think of corn as maize, but the original meaning is an edible grain or cereal. The Hebrew word for corn means "to be increased or to multiply."

D

DAIS: The platform, or raised floor, in the East of the lodge where the Master sits. In the lodge, the steps to this should be three. The Senior Warden's place should be raised two steps and that of the junior Warden, one step.

DARKNESS: Symbolizes that state of ignorance before light (knowledge) is received.

D.D.G.M: District Deputy Grand Master, an assistant who acts for the Grand Master in a particular district.

DEACON: Comes from the Greek diakonos meaning "messenger or waiting-man."

"DEDICATED TO THE MEMORY OF THE HOLY SAINTS JOHN.": Dedication is a less sacred ceremony than consecration. Hence, lodges are consecrated to God, but dedicated to patrons of the Fraternity.

DEMIT or DIMIT: A release; a resignation of membership; a paper certifying a withdrawal from a lodge (or Masonic body) when in good standing. Both spellings are used, although DIMIT is peculiar to Freemasonry only. In the U.S. some jurisdictions use the former spelling, but the majority use the latter, "Dimit."

DESTITUTE: lacking means, as without money or food.

DIGEST: Book of laws of a Grand Lodge in the U.S.; sometimes called The Code.

DISPENSATION: Permission to do that which would be forbidden otherwise.

DISTRESS: Physical or mental anguish. A brother in distress does not necessarily mean that he is without funds.

DOTAGE: An advanced age when the mind is no longer able to comprehend clearly.

DUE EAST AND WEST: Moses built the Tabernacle due east and west and this practice was carried on by the church builders. The Freemason travels from the West to the East (light) in search of a Master from whom he may gain instruction, or light,

DUE FORM: A Masonic body is opened or closed in "due form" when performed fully according to a prescribed ritual. Distinguished from "ample form."

DUE GUARD: A mode of recognition peculiar to Freemasons.

DULY AND TRULY PREPARED: That the candidate is truly prepared in his heart

and mind to receive further enlightenment; also, properly clothed, Masonically.

E

ECLIPTIC: the imaginary line followed on the earth's surface by the direct ray of the sun during the year. It makes an angle of 23' 27' with the equator. Jerusalem is located in approximately 31' 30' north attitude, that is, approximately 7' 3' north of the ecliptic.

EAR, THE ATTENTIVE OR LISTENING: The Hebrew word means not only to hear, but to understand and to obey.

EAST: From the Sun worshipers down through the ages, the East has always been considered the most honored place because the sun rises in the East and is the region from which light rises.

EAVESDROPPER: One who attempts to listen surreptitiously; literally, one standing under the eaves and thus gets only the "droppings."

EMBLEM: A representation of an idea by a visible object; a symbolical figure or design.

EMBLEMATICAL: symbolical, representing.

EMBROIDERED: having a border.

ENTERED APPRENTICE: In Operative Masonry the apprenticeship lasted seven years; if then found acceptable, the apprentice's name was entered on the books of the lodge and he was given a recognized place in the craft organization.

EUCLID: the first mathematician to Systematize the science of geometry.

EXAMINATION: the examination of a brother to determine his geniuses should not aim at displaying the committee's knowledge. It is a test of the visitor. He need not be able to answer questions from the Posting Lecture. He should know the signs, grips, and words.

EXPULSION: Forcible ejection from membership for such reasons as un-Masonic conduct, crimes, etc. It is the most severe of Masonic penalties and deprives the person of all rights and privileges formerly enjoyed from his lodge and the Fraternity as a whole.

F

FAITH. The evidence of things not seen; confidence; trust.

FAITHFUL BREAST: Symbolically, the initiate is instructed that the lessons he has received are to be treasured in his heart and remembered, and not to be forgotten; that which is told in confidence will be so held.

FELLOWCRAFT: A craftsman no longer an apprentice who has been admitted as full member, but who has not yet reached the status of a master. The Fellowcraft age represents the stage of manhood.

FEALTY: Loyalty.

FIAT LUX ET LUX FIT: Latin motto meaning "Let there be light, and there was light."

FIDELITY: faithfulness.

FIRST LANDMARKS OF MASONRY: Modes of recognition with no variation.

FORM OF A LODGE: An oblong square or parallelogram, twice as long as wide. At the time of the Temple, the only known world was the Mediterranean Sea and the countries to the north, south and east, forming an oblong. Thus, the Freemason's lodge was the world itself.

47TH PROPOSITION OF EUCLID: Derived its name from the fact that it was the 47th problem in Euclid's geometry. Sometimes called problem or theorem, which are also correct. The 47th Proposition, or problem, is to prove that in a right angled triangle, the sum of the squares of the two sides is equal to the square of the hypotenuse. Masonically, it is an emblem of the arts and sciences and reminds us that next to sinfulness, the most dangerous enemy of life is ignorance.

FRATERNITY: A brotherhood, in which blood-bonds are replaced by a common devotion to a principle, code, or creed.

FREE BORN: A free soul; one having attained mastery of himself by self discipline. It is a misconception that this refers to one not born into slavery.

FREEMASONS: The early builders in Operative Masonry times were free men, not serfs or bondsmen and were free to move from one place to another as their work demanded. Thus, they came to be called "Freemasons."

FURNISHINGS OF A LODGE: Holy Bible, Square and Compasses, Charter or Dispensation.

G

"G": The letter -G- is the Saxon representative of the Hebrew Yod and the Greek Tau; The initial letter of the name of the Eternal in those languages. It stands not only for God, but for Geometry, that science so important to all Freemasons.

G.A.O.T.U.: Grand Architect of the Universe.

GAVEL: Derives its name from its shape-that of the gable or gavel end of a house. It is a tool used by a stonemason and resembles a hammer having a pointed end for cutting. The Working Tool gavel differs from the upright gavel, or "Hiram." (See Hiram.)

GOD: The Hebrew words for Beauty, Strength, and Wisdom (the supports of Freemasonry) are Gomer, Oz, and Dabar. The initials of these words compose the English name of the Deity.

GRAND EAST: The place where the Grand Lodge holds its communications and from which place the edicts are issued.

GREAT LIGHTS: The Holy Bible, Square and Compasses. The Bible represents the will of God, the Square is the physical life of man and the Compasses represents the moral and spiritual life.

GRIPS: Every brother following his raising should be taught to start with the grip of an Entered Apprentice Mason and go through the grips, passes, and words to the Grand Masonic Word.

GUILD (GILD) MASONS. GUTTURAL: From the Latin guttur meaning "the throat."

H

HISTORICAL: According to history, verifiable, capable of documentary proof. We also speak of traditional and legendary history, meaning popular belief, not upheld by fact.

HOMAGE: respect, as applied to men; worship, as applied to deity.

HOUR GLASS: Emblem of life.

HEALED: Obligated in a degree which the Mason has not had conferred on him. To "heal" is to "make valid."

HELE: Pronounced "hail" and means to keep guarded, or secret. Sometimes spelled "hale."

HEMISPHERE: Half of the earth's surface, as the western hemisphere, the northern hemisphere.

HIEROGLYPHICS: Literally the symbols in the priestly writings of the Egyptians. Generally, a symbol or sign the meaning of which is known only to the initiated.

HIRAM: An upright gavel made in the form of a maul and used by a presiding officer.

H.K.T: Hiram, King of Tyre.

HOODWINK: A blindfold which is a symbol of secrecy; mystical darkness.

HOUR GLASS: An emblem of the passage of time.

I

ILL. OR ILLUSTRIOUS: A title used in addressing members of the 33rd.

ILLUSTRATE: Giving or showing an example.

ILLUSTRATION: A drawing, picture, or example.

ILLUSTRATIVE: Showing by example or picture.

INDISCRIMINATELY: Without distinction between.

I.N.R.I: Jesus Nazarenus, Rex Iudworum, meaning "Jesus of Nazareth, King of the Jews."

INTELLIGIBLE: Capable of being read or understood

J

JACHIN: Comes from two Hebrew words meaning "God will establish." The right hand pillar of the porch of King Solomon's Temple.

JACOB'S LADDER: Symbol of progress from earth to heaven.

JEWELS, MOVABLE AND IMMOVABLE: The Movable jewels are the Rough and Perfect Ashlars and the Trestle Board and are so called because they are not confined to any particular part of the lodge whereas the Immovable jewels: the Square, Level, and Plumb, have definite locations. They are called "jewels" not because of their materials, but because of their meaning. The word "jewel" comes from the Greek meaning "bright or shining."

K

KORAN, THE: The Sacred Volume of Mohammedan Law.

L

LAMB: "In all ages the Lamb has been deemed an emblem of innocence." The candidate is therefore given a white lambskin apron.

LANDMARKS: Ancient and universal customs of the Order which gradually grew into operation as rules of action.

LAWFUL AGE: A man of discretion.

LAWFUL INFORMATION: That one has tested by trial and examination, or knows that such has been done by another.

LEGALLY CONSTITUTED: A Lodge working under proper authority and Charter from a Grand Lodge.

LEGENDARY: according to popular belief or report, but without proof. A legend usually carries with it the idea of the miraculous.

LEGIBLE: Capable of being read.

LIBERAL ARTS AND SCIENCES: Grammar, Rhetoric, Logic, Arithmetic, Geometry, Music, and Astronomy.

LILY-WORK: Emblem of peace and unity.

LODGE OF THE HOLY SAINTS JOHN OF JERUSALEM and LODGE OF ST. JOHN: Masonic tradition has it that the primitive, or mother, Lodge was held at Jerusalem and dedicated to St. John the Baptist, and then to St. John the Evangelist, and finally to both. This Lodge was therefore called "The Lodge of the Holy Saints John of Jerusalem." From this Lodge all other Lodges are supposed, figuratively, to descend.

LOST WORD: That for which the Mason search is to discover the divine in himself and in the world that he might achieve mental satisfaction and ultimate happiness.

LOW TWELVE: The hour of midnight; darkness is a symbol of death as well as of ignorance.

LUX E TENEBRIS: Latin meaning "Light out of darkness."

M

MAKING A MASON "AT SIGHT": By a Grand Master's prerogative, some constitutional requirement is set aside-usually the ballot, and a man is made a Master Mason without waiting or instruction between degrees.

MASONIC AGES: The age of an Entered Apprentice is said to be three years (the symbol of peace or perfect harmony); that of a Fellowcraft, five years (the symbol of active life); and that of a Master Mason, seven years (the symbol of perfection).

MERIDIAN: The position of the sun at noon.

MORIAH: A hill in Jerusalem on which the Temple of Solomon was built.

MOSAIC PAVEMENT: Tessellated pavement or checkered floor. An inlay floor composed of black and white squares.

MOUTH TO EAR: The method whereby the esoteric work of Freemasonry is passed on from one Mason to another, or from one Mason to the candidate who is qualified to receive such information.

MYSTIC TIE: Spiritual tie not easily broken; fellowship among Masons.

N

NEITHER NAKED NOR CLOTHED: Neither unclothed, or defenseless, nor clothed and self-sufficient.

NOBLES: Members of the Mystic Shrine.

O

OATH: A solemn affirmation, in the name of God, that what one testifies is true.

OBLIGATION: A promise or pledge of obedience. The Mason takes an obligation, not an oath, that he will not depart from the promises he makes.

OBLONG SQUARE: A right angle with one side longer than the other.

ORALLY: Aloud, spoken.

ORIENTAL CHAIR: The seat of the Master in the East; the Oriental Chair of King Solomon.

ORNAMENTS OF A LODGE: The Mosaic Pavement, Indented Tessel, and Blazing Star.

ORNAN: Name of Jebusite from whom David purchased a threshing floor in Jerusalem in which King Solomon's temple was built. This was previously the site of the alter.

P

PAST: A term applied in Masonry to an officer who has held an office for the term for which he was elected, and has then retired, as Past Master, Past Senior Grand Warden.

PASSING THE CHAIR: The ceremony of installation of the presiding officer.

PECTORAL: Pertaini breast.

PEDESTALS: The columns before the Master and Wardens of a lodge.

PERFECT AHSLAR: Every Mason is expected to perfect or "polish" himself in building his character in order that he may become acceptable in the sight of God and be fit to take his rightful place in the finished work of Masonry

PERFECT LODGE: One which contains the constitutional number of members.

PERFECT POINTS OF ENTRANCE: Symbolic action called for on entrance into a lodge.

PERFECT SQUARE: A right angle with the sides equal.

PHARAOH: The title of the ruler of ancient Egypt.

PHILALETHES: Friends of truth.

PLANETARY: Pertaining to the planets.

PLUMB: An instrument for erecting perpendiculars.

PLUMB LINE: The Working Tool of a Past Master; the perfect emblem of uprightness.

POTENTATE: A ruler, sovereign, or monarch.

POT OF INCENSE: Signifies that, of all forms of worship, it is more acceptable to God to be pure and blameless in our inner lives than anything else.

PROFANE: A non-Mason, The word comes from the Latin pro meaning "before" and Janum meaning "a temple." Hence, in Masonry it means those who have not been in the Temple, that is, initiated.

PROFICIENT: Means not only proficient in the ritualistic work, but before the world in daily living.

Q
R

REFRESHMENT: Rest period symbolized by noon.

REGULAR LODGE: One working under a charter or warrant from a legal authority.

REPRIMAND: One of the Masonic penalties which can be and is enforced to reprove.

RITUAL: Comes from the Latin ritualist meaning "ceremonial forms."

ROUGH ASHLAR: The unenlightened member; man in his natural state before being educated.

S

SANCTUM SANCTORUM: Latin for "Holy of Holies."

SECRETS: Masonry's only secrets are in its methods of recognition and of symbolic instructions. Its principles and aims have never been secret.

SHIBBOLETH: An ear of corn; a test word; a watchword; slogan.

SIGNS, MASONIC: Modes of recognition often serving as a reminder of some event or pledge.

SOLSTICE: The point in the ecliptic at which the sun is farthest from the equator (north in summer, south in winter).

SONS OF LIGHT: During the building of King Solomon's Temple the Masons were so called.

SPECULATIVE MASONRY: Freemasonry in its modern acceptance; the application of the implements of Operative masonry to a system of ethics.

SPRIG OF ACACIA: Symbolizes the immortality of the soul.

STATIONS AND PLACES: Officers are elected to stations and appointed to places.

SUMMONS: A notification from the Master to appear. For its neglect, because it comes directly under the province of his obligation, a member may be disciplined and/or punished.

SUSPENSION: Temporary privation of power or rights, such as suspension for nonpayment of dues. One of the Masonic penalties.

SWORD POINTING TO THE NAKED HEART: Signifies that justice is one of the most rigorous laws and if we are unjust in our hearts, the center of our being, the inevitable result of injustice will find us out.

SYMBOL: Signifies or represents some truth, idea or fact, but is not itself the thing it represents.

SYMBOL OF GLORY: The Blazing Star in the old lectures. The star in the center represented Deity, hence, the "Symbol of Glory."

T

TENETS OF FREEMASONRY: Dogmas; principles, beliefs, doctrines; teachings of Brotherly Love, Relief and Truth. A Tenet is something obviously true; that which is universally accepted without question.

TERRESTRIAL: Belonging to the earth.

TESSELLATED PAVEMENT: Checkered floor of black and white, symbolic of the triumphs and the despairs throughout life.

TETRAGRAMMATON: A Greek word signifying "four letters.' It is a name given by the Talmudists when referring to God or Jehovah.

TOKEN, MASONIC: A sign used for recognition to prove that a man is a Mason.

"TO THAT UNDISCOVERED COUNTRY FROM WHOSE BOURNE NO TRAVELER RETURNS": Comes from Shakespeare's Hamlet (Act III, Scene 1).

TRACING BOARD: Or emblematic chart. Emblems used to illustrate the lectures.

TRADITIONAL: According to a belief handed down from generation to generation, but not supported by any sure or exact evidence. A tradition need have nothing of the miraculous in it.

TRANSITION: The passing over from one stage to another.

TRAVELING FROM WEST TO EAST: In Operative Masonry workmen traveled from one job to another and the word "traveling" came to signify a form of work. Hence, a Mason works his way toward the East (place of light) by improving himself as he progresses through life.

THREE STEPS: Emblematical of youth, manhood, and age.

TRESTLE BOARD: The carpet or board upon which the Master inscribes the designs for guidance of the Craft. In the present day it refers to the meeting notice sent to the membership.

TRIALS, MASONIC: Are held in Masonic courts of law in which testimony is heard and the accused either found innocent or guilty.

TROWEL: The Working Tool of the Master Mason. Symbolically, to spread the cement of Brotherly Love to fit the capstone to complete the building.

TUBAL CAIN: Artificer in brass and iron. The first Master Craftsman, son of Lamech and Zillah. See Genesis IV:22.

TYRE: City of Sidonian Empire which is only 120 miles by sea from Jerusalem. King Hiram or Tyre provided materials for the building of the Temple.

U

UN-MASONIC CONDUCT: Conduct of a Mason which violates the laws of the Craft and his obligation thereto.

V

VISITING: To visit a lodge outside of your "regular" lodge. Visitation Is a privilege and not a right.

V.S.L: Volume of the Sacred Law.

VOUCHING: A brother cannot vouch for the Masonic standing of a brother unless he has sat with him in a Masonic Lodge. Knowledge of his standing or membership in a body requiring Masonic membership as a prerequisite is not grounds for avouchment.

VOID: Empty.

W

WARDENS COLUMNS: At the beginning of the opening ceremonies both columns are down, The Senior Warden's column is elevated down when the WM declares the Lodge open. It is lowered when the Master declares the Lodge called from labor to refreshment, or when, ill the closing ceremonies. The Junior Warden's column is elevated up, when the Lodge is at refreshment. It raised at the moment when the Master declares the Lodge at refreshment, and is lowered when he calls the Lodge to labor. The Senior Warden's column is lowered and raised at the same times.

WAGES, A MASTER'S: Symbolizing the fruits of a man's labors in Masonic work.

WINDING STAIRS: Is one which tries a man's soul. He must approach it with faith believing that there is a top, that by a long and arduous climb he will reach a Middle Chamber. A place of light,

WORKING TOOL OF A PAST MASTER: The plumb line.

WORSHIPFUL: Title of honor and respect.

WORTHY AND WELL QUALIFIED: That by his character and moral living, the candidate is worthy to be a member.

X

Y

YEAR, MASONIC: While the civil calendar reckons from the Year of our Lord and is designated A.D., the Masonic calendar dates from the year when God said, "Let there be Light," and is designated A. L.

YOD: The tenth letter of the Hebrew alphabet.

YORK RITE: The degrees of the lodge, chapter, council, and commandery.

Z

ZEAL: Intensity of purpose and of earnestness.

ZEND-AVESTA: The Persian Volume of the Sacred Law.

ZENITH: The point in heavens directly over head of the spectator; great height.

ZION: The mountain or hill in Palestine on which Jerusalem was built.

NOTES:

NOTES:

www.ingramcontent.com/pod-product-compliance
Lightning Source LLC
Chambersburg PA
CBHW061357280526
45784CB00001B/289